The British Partisan

The British Partisan

Capture, Imprisonment and Escape in Wartime Italy

Michael Ross

Pen & Sword
MILITARY

First published in Great Britain in 1997 by Minerva Press as
From Liguria with Love – Capture, Imprisonment and Escape in Wartime Italy
Republished in this format in 2019 by
Pen & Sword Military
An imprint of
Pen & Sword Books Ltd
Yorkshire – Philadelphia

ISBN 978 1 52675 035 8

Typeset by Mac Style
Printed and bound in the UK by TJ International Ltd,
Padstow, Cornwall

Pen & Sword Books Limited incorporates the imprints of Atlas,
Archaeology, Aviation, Discovery, Family History, Fiction, History,
Maritime, Military, Military Classics, Politics, Select, Transport, True
Crime, Air World, Frontline Publishing, Leo Cooper, Remember When,
Seaforth Publishing, The Praetorian Press, Wharncliffe Local History,
Wharncliffe Transport, Wharncliffe True Crime and White Owl.

For a complete list of Pen & Sword titles please contact

PEN & SWORD BOOKS LIMITED
47 Church Street, Barnsley, South Yorkshire, S70 2AS, England
E-mail: enquiries@pen-and-sword.co.uk
Website: www.pen-and-sword.co.uk

Or
PEN AND SWORD BOOKS
1950 Lawrence Rd, Havertown, PA 19083, USA
E-mail: Uspen-and-sword@casematepublishers.com
Website: www.penandswordbooks.com

To Giovanna, David, Stephen and Alessandra

Contents

List of Maps

List of Illustrations

Preface

Do the work that's nearest,
Though it's dull at whiles,
Helping, when we meet them,
Lame dogs over stiles.

Charles Kingsley

It is now many years since the Second World War and the events which I describe in the following pages. Over the course of time, some of my memories have faded beyond recall, but the ones recounted here, written in the immediate post-war period, remain vivid and, I am confident, form a true record of my experiences during that fateful period.

My original purpose was to provide my children with an account of my personal involvement in those events. Now, much later, having combined the writings into a single book – helped by my daughter Alessandra's painstaking checking of the scripts – I hope that others may read it too. I should like to think that, in its own small way, it might contribute to a better understanding and appreciation of peoples of other lands.

Like me, there must be many who have found themselves 'lame dogs' at some time in their lives, dependent on the compassion of others. I consider myself fortunate indeed to have met so many people ready to help me over the 'stiles' when I came to them.

Throughout these writings I have used the real names of those involved. In two instances only, Palmero and Bruno, I thought it wise to use fictitious ones. But there were countless others, strangers whose names I shall never know, who gave help and protection with no thought of reward and often at grave personal risk.

Strange though it may seem, my wartime experiences have left me with an unshakeable faith in the fundamental goodness of mankind.

Michael Ross, London, 1997.

Introduction

The war in Africa was in its second year. Following Mussolini's declaration of war in 1940, General Wavell's British forces based in Egypt and the Sudan attacked and overran the Italian colonies of Abyssinia and Eritria and advanced well into Libya, Mussolini's last stronghold. But the promising Libyan operation ground to a halt when Wavell was required to divert troops to Greece and Crete in an ill-fated attempt to defend them against German forces advancing from central Europe. Then, to compound Wavell's problems, the Germans under General Rommel landed in North Africa for the first time. The combined German-Italian armies forced the British Eighth Army to relinquish its gains in Libya and retreat back to Egypt.

The Axis advance was halted, enabling reinforcements of men and materials to be rushed to Egypt. I was among them, part of a contingent of five other officers and two hundred men of the Welch Regiment. We had been sent to make good the losses suffered by our 1st Welch Battalion in Crete.

Like most of the others, I was in my early twenties and fresh from the training camps at home, glad of a reprieve from endless mock battles and exercises. Months of intensive training had hardened us and rendered us, supposedly, impatient for 'real action'.

After arrival we passed the first few weeks savouring the luxury of social life in the safety of the Citadel, an ancient fortress overlooking the metropolis of Cairo, before being plunged into the rigours and tedium of desert training. Meanwhile, there was a change of command; General Wavell had gone to India to be replaced by General Auchinleck, who within two months had launched us into a new Libyan offensive.

It was November 1941, and within a month of the reopening of hostilities Rommel's defences had collapsed and his army was on the run. Successful tank battles cleared the way for us to advance rapidly. Tobruk and Bardia, where the besieged Australians had been holding out, were relieved, and beyond them a major prize, the port of Benghazi, fell into our hands. The enemy had beaten a hasty retreat, out of sight, and apart from occasional strafing and bombing, we were unaware of his existence.

This was hailed as a great victory throughout the Commonwealth. For the very first time in this war, German soldiers had been put to flight by British arms. Our Navy, of course, had enjoyed success against Germans in the River Plate and our Air Force at the Battle of Britain. Now at long last the Army had proved itself. The self-respect of the British soldier abroad had been restored and the spirits of the long-suffering people at home had been raised.

Although the Axis had suffered a defeat in Libya, the end of the campaign was not in sight. Rommel had kept his force largely intact at the expense of surrendering territory. The Eighth Army's lightning advance of 300 miles had left in its train extensive and vulnerable lines of communication and supply which could not be strengthened overnight. Auchinleck needed a breathing space, and Rommel, too, was glad of a respite to regroup. Hence a lull in operations.

Part I

A Soldier

Chapter 1

Despatch to a Desert Fort

It was Christmas Day 1941, with the Eighth Army somewhere in the Libyan desert. There had been a long pause in hostilities, and on a clear sunny morning in the presence of a small group of men in my company, fellow Catholics, I held a short service of prayer. I read the gospel of the Nativity – we were not far removed from the site of the original – yet somehow it all seemed a bit out of place. The men listened in silence; at least on that day it was a link with home.

We had reason to give thanks, for in under two months the Eighth Army had driven the German-Italian forces deep into Libya and lifted the threat to Egypt, our main base. One third of the country was back in our hands. Our gains included the large port of Benghazi, and it was to this place that our battalion of the Welch Regiment, with others, had received orders to proceed.

We did not baulk at this. In place of tents and bivouacs, we were back to barrack huts, iron bedsteads and running water. Less popularly, however, we were also back to tiresome training schedules. But it proved to be brief.

By 15 January we were on the move once more. Our destination was Fort Sceleidima, an uninhabited location in the open desert 50 miles south of Benghazi. Our orders were to occupy the place and hold it.

It lay in the now wide expanse of no-man's-land which had been opened up by the enemy's rapid retreat westwards. At Sceleidima we would be among the forward elements of the Eighth Army. We estimated the main body of the enemy to be 100 miles or so away. In desert conditions, however, that distance could be covered in a few hours.

Although the disengagement of the enemy had been forced upon them by their recent defeats, the campaign had taken its toll on us too. The fact that we had given up the chase suggested that we were stretched to the limit and in need of reinforcements. The enemy, though, had always to be kept guessing, and probing missions of the kind in which we were now engaged might serve to confuse them.

* * *

We left Benghazi on a sunny morning in a long convoy of vehicles under command of Colonel Napier, our battalion CO. We numbered about 400 men, some 200 having been left behind on garrison duties. Escorting the convoy was an anti-tank company commanded by me, consisting of nine guns each mounted on its own motor vehicle called a portee. These guns would be the convoy's only protection against attack by enemy armoured units as we had no tanks in close support.

Once clear of Benghazi we were on to the rough, dusty surface of the desert. Away to the east, on our left, was a high escarpment rising above the surrounding desert. This was the perimeter of a fertile region lying behind it called the Jebel Akhdar (The Green Mountain).

This escarpment ran due south for some 50 miles. It was cliff-like in parts and terminated at the extreme southern corner of the plateau. According to our maps, it was at this point that our objective, Sceleidima, was to be found. Beyond it was only desert.

The navigating officer steered the convoy towards this feature. On reaching it we picked up a firm, well-worn track winding its way due south along the foot of this high ground.

Our convoy laboured cautiously along this track skirting the escarpment towering above us on our left. On our right lay the open desert stretching as far as the eye could see, shimmering and gleaming.

My nine gun portees drove in single column on the right flank of the convoy of vehicles, keeping parallel to it. It was on this open side that any encounter with the enemy was likely to occur. We were venturing into no-man's-land, so a strict watch was kept for signs of anything unusual. I was in the leading portee and halted the jolting vehicle from time to time to gaze long and hard through my binoculars at the horizon. A low cloud of dust would have betrayed enemy movement, but none appeared, and by late afternoon on a warm, cloudless day we reached the fort without incident.

* * *

Of the fort itself there were few traces – a broken tower or two and some crumbling walls. Centuries before, it had been an outpost of the Roman and Islamic empires. It was easy to see why this site had been chosen: it was perched in an elevated position on the extreme corner of the plateau with uninterrupted views of the approaches across the lower-lying desert to the south and west.

Behind the fort the Jebel Akhdar stretched 50 miles north to the Mediterranean coast and 100 miles east before meeting the desert again. Resembling a hilly island in a sea of sand, it comprised an area of bush and scrub with grass and trees in its more fertile parts, and was the homeland of wandering Senussi tribes.

Beyond the horizon to our front, somewhere in the open expanses, mobile columns of the Guards Armoured Brigade were known to be operating. This was some comfort to us as we were conscious of being probably the nearest ground troops to the main body of the enemy.

After arrival we followed the usual routine of orders and briefings, posting of sentries, despatch of patrols, selection of firing positions, digging of protective trenches and unloading of stores. My first task was the offloading of the guns and siting them around the front of the fort. Then came the domestic chores, dispersal of the men in bivouac areas, digging of latrines and preparation of meals. Every moment of what was left of daylight was spent in improving our camouflage and acquainting ourselves with the layout of the area, before settling down to the first night's vigil.

* * *

It proved a peaceful night, and when dawn came we resumed the task of building our defences. Patrolling the danger zone continued day and night but resulted invariably in 'Nothing to report'. The days passed, but the situation remained unchanged.

Morale, however, was still high. Men had long since felt a special pride in belonging to the Eighth Army and perhaps even a touch of romanticism about campaigning in the desert.

Unlike the battles waged through densely populated Europe in 1940, with their aftermath of human misery, those in North Africa had been fought over vast empty stretches of desert wastes devoid of habitation. Such terrain, lacking roads, shelter and water, was neutral; there was no third human element to help or hinder the combatants.

These were times when the leaders of both sides enforced strict codes of conduct and discipline, reflected in the humane treatment of prisoners and especially of the wounded. The enemy was spoken of in respectful terms. The shrewdness of Rommel and the skill at arms of his soldiers were fully acknowledged. Rommel himself had become a legend – it was customary for us to refer to the enemy simply as 'Rommel', something our High Command thought fit expressly to forbid, albeit in vain.

Identification with the enemy was not surprising; men on both sides were in a strange landscape far removed from home; loneliness and isolation were felt by friend and foe alike; we endured the same hardships of life in a barren desert, as well as sharing the joys of its occasional beauty.

Comparison could be drawn with the fellowship evidenced among the combatants on the Western Front of the First World War: those men lived and died in a unique world known only to themselves. Jon's cartoons of the Eighth Army's 'Two Types' in Libya shared a kindred spirit with Bruce Bainsfather's 'Ole Bill' in Flanders a quarter of a century earlier.

The battle zone was itself confined within clearly defined boundaries, the sea to the north, the forbidding soft sands to the south, whilst to the east and west lay the safe base areas, ours at Cairo and the Axis's at Tripoli. These bases were like havens, essential to the preparation and launching of offensives, just as seaports were to the conduct of naval operations. In both cases, the further one ventured from them the greater the problems of supply, communications and security.

There were many ways in which conditions in the desert bore resemblance to those on the high seas. Landmarks were few or negligible, making navigation by compass common. The vagaries of the elements could bear as hard upon the desert soldier as on the sailor. Sandstorms, reducing visibility to zero, could blow up suddenly and, like gales or fog at sea, curtail activity for days on end. Soldiers hated them; the fine dust stuck to their faces like brown make-up, while the grit penetrated everything, including food and drink.

Desert fighting units, like warships, had to be mobile and self-contained. In between planned offensives there were periods when contact with the enemy could be lost altogether, and if chance encounters occurred they were usually short and sharp. The small, specially equipped units of our Long Range Desert Group would embark on missions deep into enemy territory, make surprise attacks on selected targets, submarine-fashion, then hasten back to base, relying on speed and camouflage to outwit and escape the enemy.

This analogy between sea and desert warfare held good in the field of strategy. The mere acquisition and occupation of desert lands, like parts of the ocean, could be meaningless. Indeed, it could be an unwanted liability. Both sides had long since learned that ultimate victory would go to the one that succeeded in trapping the opposing forces and capturing or destroying them. Only then could the war in North Africa be brought to an end and the territories permanently secured.

Chapter 2

Enemy Threats

It was a week since we had taken up positions around the fort. Life had been peaceful, and the silence was broken only by occasional distant explosions, no doubt the work of hit-and-run aircraft raiding supply lines. Nevertheless, vigilance was essential and sentries kept continuous watch round the clock. The enemy on the ground was still remote and unseen, but one morning we received a sharp reminder that he was indeed there, lurking just beyond our horizon. It was an incident involving two of our Bren gun carriers. These were small, fast, tracked vehicles with some armour plating, but open on top. They carried four or five men and were very suitable for reconnaissance missions. A pair of them was sent out every day to probe the area well ahead of our position.

One morning when far afield, they suddenly encountered two enemy light tanks and came under fire from their cannon. The carriers, armed only with machine guns, wisely sought to escape as quickly as possible. The enemy gave chase and during the skirmish one of the carriers was halted by a direct hit. The second carrier was unable to go to its assistance as the tanks were closing in on it. On reaching the stricken carrier, the enemy gave up the pursuit, presumably deciding they had ventured far enough. This enabled our second carrier to get back safely and tell the tale.

It was during the hours of darkness, however, that the enemy would bestir himself like some nocturnal animal awakening and make his presence known. The blackness of the sky would frequently be disturbed by distant ground flashes illuminating temporarily the cloud formations above. Occasionally an aircraft would be seen to ignite in the sky and fall slowly and silently with a trail of fire.

More common was the sight of a succession of coloured signal lights which the enemy would shoot up into the sky at regular intervals as markers for their mobile columns. The movement of these roving columns could be easily followed by the changing position of the lights. It was difficult to judge how far away they were, but at times they seemed to be advancing well into our territory and, more disconcertingly, on all sides. The dawn, however, would reveal no trace of these nightly apparitions.

By contrast, the daylight hours passed uneventfully and we busied ourselves digging and camouflaging and generally making ourselves more secure and comfortable. As usual during times of inactivity, there was much speculation about the immediate future. Conflicting rumours spread among the soldiery which, we used to say, was a pretty sure indicator that Army Headquarters was uncertain about the next move too. Private Thomas, my batman, was convinced that Richie, the Eighth Army commander, was all for pressing on, while Auchinleck, the overall commander in the Middle East, favoured a period of consolidation. Dai Morgan, the company cook, had been assured by an RASC corporal delivering the rations that the Welch were to be taken out of the line and sent back to Alexandria for garrison duties – the soldier's pipe dream. But whatever the options, a big decision was imminent, as we learned that Auchinleck had just flown up to Benghazi to confer with Richie.

The conjecture and speculation, however, were soon set aside when suddenly and quite unexpectedly we came face to face with the realities of the situation.

* * *

It happened one hot afternoon when a lookout, peering through the haze with his binoculars, sighted a solitary figure far off in the open desert staggering about aimlessly. A section of men was sent out to investigate.

It turned out to be a British officer, a major of the Queen's Bays, so mentally and physically exhausted that he had to be helped back to our lines. He was tall, slightly built, with fair hair but balding; not a young man. His features were drawn and his eyes lifeless, a victim of shock.

Later that evening, after he had slept, he took some food in our mess vehicle. We were naturally eager to ply him with questions, but his responses were slow and laboured and it was not easy to make sense of what he mumbled. Apparently his armoured squadron had been engaged by the enemy and his own tank had been hit and set on fire. He managed to extricate himself but was the only one of his crew to survive. He had been wandering for two days so was lucky to have stumbled upon our detachment. I do not think he could have gone much further.

From what else he said one thing became clear: our tanks had been engaged in large numbers and had suffered a serious defeat. This was our first inkling of the crucial events of the previous few days. Only later were we to hear the whole story.

We learned that between 23 and 25 January a trial of strength between the armoured forces of both sides had taken place. The German Panzer Division, with its acknowledged superiority in armoured fighting vehicles, was involved in a number of widespread encounters with British mobile units, including the newly arrived and inexperienced 1 Armoured Division.

There had been much confusion and differences of opinion between the British commanders regarding the best course of action to be taken. The ensuing indecision and delays had been quickly seized upon by Rommel and used to his advantage. The result had been a series of crippling defeats for our forward armoured units. The loss of tanks was critical; they are the teeth of an army. Just as an animal without teeth cannot long survive in the jungle, so an army without tanks cannot hope to do so in battle.

Perhaps this state of confusion was to blame for some contradictory orders that we had ourselves received the day before the arrival of the fugitive tank officer. We were told to pull back immediately to Regima, a town some 50 miles to the north in the Jebel Akhdar region. So we packed up and left, but when only half way we received countermanding orders telling us to get straight back to Sceleidima.

The facts gleaned at first hand from our visitor provided a realistic if cheerless assessment of the situation. He left us in a returning ration truck after a night's rest, but the ill tidings he had brought remained with us. There seemed little prospect now of the much vaunted spring offensive by the Eighth Army. Rommel had grasped the initiative, and the chances were that we would be obliged to stay put and wait for the enemy storm to break upon us.

Ominous signs of what was in store were soon forthcoming. Late that afternoon, towards the east, came the sound of unusually heavy explosions. They continued after dark so we were able to time the interval between the flash and the boom – the sort of thing one did as a child during thunderstorms. From this we calculated them to be 30 miles away at a place we judged must be Msus.

Msus was one of our manned outposts guarding a forward petrol and ammunition dump. We could only conclude that either the enemy was attacking the place or else our sappers were deliberately blowing up the dump to prevent it falling into enemy hands Whatever was going on, there could be no doubt now that Rommel was on the move.

* * *

After a day of intermittent rain and grey haze, dawn on the 27th was bright. The clouds had dispersed, leaving a clear sky and crisp air. A mid-morning bucket of tea had just arrived from the company cookhouse and was being ladled into the dixies of the waiting soldiers. The usual exchange of views on the quality of the brew followed. Occasionally it would be salty, more frequently it had a smell of petrol – attributed to lack of discrimination by cookhouse orderlies when utilizing empty cans. But today's issue was given general approval. 'Great, boyo', was how Dai Jones, the signaller, rated it.

The tonic effect of tea, whether real or imagined, was undeniable. For me, alas, cookhouse tea did nothing. Only once since leaving the comfort of the officer's mess at the Citadel in Cairo had I really relished it. The occasion was one evening when, calling on an Indian officer colleague, he offered me his speciality: a tall engraved silver beaker of sweet tea made with hot milk. Sipping this nectar while watching one of those staggeringly beautiful desert sunsets was something to remember. Morning char at Sceleidima was never like that!

Monty Champion, the second-in-command, was approaching with his usual heavy step. On reaching our gathering, the musical chatter of the Welshmen abated as Monty called out, 'Tea all right?' He waited for the customary reassuring response before peering into the bucket for final confirmation. Satisfied that all was well, he strolled over to where I was standing and took me to one side. He hit a stone with his walking stick, golf fashion, then glancing up mumbled, 'The Bosch is in Msus!'

He moved off without waiting for my reaction. I was reminded of the occasion three months earlier when he had come up to me at half time on the rugger pitch at Gezira Sporting Club in Cairo and said in the same brusque manner, 'We need more fight from the threes!' and then stalked off, sucking a lemon.

* * *

The fall of Msus was certainly bad news for us. The troops there had been the nearest ones on our left flank. On our right flank there had been no units anyway, so this meant we were now on our own, out on a limb.

We were clearly one of the enemy's next objectives. Sceleidima straddled the main track skirting the escarpment along which his columns would pass en route for Benghazi, a vital sea port and the major prize in these parts.

Although the front was in a state of flux, we received no further information that day and no fresh orders. Our duty, therefore, was simply to stand our ground and deny it to the enemy if challenged.

We wondered how important Command Headquarters regarded the holding of Sceleidima, since no mines or wiring had been supplied. We had a sneaking feeling that in the confusion and disorder caused by Rommel's sudden aggression a general withdrawal was taking place and our small detachment had been overlooked – or worse, written off.

Even the enemy kept us guessing. There was as yet no sign or sight of him, at least not during the day. But that night the customary display of distant coloured lights being shot up into the sky from time to time by moving columns turned out to be a veritable firework spectacular. The lights seemed to be everywhere and continued relentlessly for hours. Rommel was regrouping in earnest for a major offensive. An attack was imminent.

Chapter 3

The Storm Breaks

It was the early hours of Tuesday, 28 January and still dark. The muted orders 'Stand to' had brought weary soldiers silently from their bivouacs and potholes to take up defensive positions around our lines and prepare to repulse the traditional dawn attack. This state of alert, lasting one hour, was a daily drill, strictly observed and continued until daylight, when the welcome order 'Stand down' rang out.

This morning, our vigil over and still feeling the chill of the night in our bones, we were glad to stand up and anticipate the pleasant glow of the sun's first rays. Men well wrapped and with woollen balaclavas pulled down over their ears were swinging their arms across their bodies and stamping their feet to keep the circulation going. Tea was quickly dispensed around the groups of soldiers standing about talking in low voices or lighting cigarettes. Some crouched on the ground with collars upturned sucking the hot drink from mess tins cradled in their hands for warmth.

I could not help feeling that this, surely, was to be a day of destiny for many of these men uprooted from the black and green valleys of the Welsh mountains and transposed to this grey alien desert, a desert where some had already found a permanent resting place.

The hardships and discipline of their Welsh valley upbringing had given these men a special resilience in withstanding discomfort and tedium. Their national pride and love of home found expression in the frequent singing of the hymns of their native land. They were warm-hearted, generous and endowed with a ready sense of humour. They refused to be unduly elated by success, and were equally undaunted by misfortune.

The Welshman could live up to his reputation of being fiery when roused, but otherwise he was a quiet soul. If anything, as a soldier he lacked aggression, but this was more than compensated for by his resolution, endurance, and loyalty. Though not Welsh myself, I would not have wished to serve with any other regiment.

* * *

The chilly dawn that day was soon transformed into a beautifully warm morning. The carrier patrols set off as usual at sunrise. They headed in the direction of Msus and quickly disappeared behind the broken ground. The rest of us, having completed ablutions and feeding, settled down to the daily routine of weapon maintenance, improving our cover and camouflage and, above all, keeping watch for the enemy.

The morning hours were passing by uneventfully until suddenly at about 11.00 we were surprised by the reappearance of our carriers racing back to base at full speed. They were not expected for another hour. Something unusual must have happened.

They were soon flying through our lines in a cloud of dust. Lewis, the carrier officer, was standing in the leading vehicle. As he passed me he raised his arms with outstretched fingers indicating large numbers of enemy approaching. There was a half smile on his flushed face as he went by.

Almost immediately the order 'Stand to' could be heard echoing around the lines, causing soldiers to scamper to firing positions and the protection of trenches, while vehicles were moved to the rear out of the way.

As yet, there was no sign of the enemy, but by using the broken ground on our left flank they would be able to get fairly close to us without being seen.

Waiting for an unseen enemy who you know is creeping up on you can be eerie. I felt a quickening of heartbeat and a tingling sensation on the tip of my tongue. Those around me were suddenly serious; their banter and chirpiness had been silenced.

Of my nine guns, three were with me under voice control in a forward position; the remaining six were sited in depth nearer the escarpment. The guns themselves were the 37mm Bofors anti-tank gun, a light, mobile weapon with a 5ft barrel mounted on a pair of wheels. They could be manhandled short distances but otherwise were towed behind a portee or winched up on top of the vehicle. At this moment our portees were parked in the rear.

The Bofors had been successful in the early campaigns, but the ever increasing strength of tank armour had reduced their effectiveness. A replacement weapon, the two-pounder, on which we had already been trained, was on its way to us. Meanwhile, we had to rely on the old Bofors.

* * *

The anxious moments of waiting were short-lived. Very soon the air above was filled with the sounds of screeching shells passing straight over us and landing with cracking explosions on the escarpment behind. There was a short respite, but then came another salvo, followed by another and another. The war was back.

Apprehension showed on the faces of the men around me, but spirits rose as the ineffectiveness of the enemy shelling became apparent. Our troops were well dispersed about Sceleidema and, short of a direct hit, were safe in their slit trenches.

The shelling continued for some fifteen minutes before easing off. No casualties had so far been suffered in my lines. However, mortar bombs now joined the fray, falling uncomfortably near. This was a sure sign that the enemy was drawing closer, as mortars are carried and fired by infantrymen at short range. It also meant that we were probably under observation, although from where we were we could see no sign of the enemy yet.

In order to be forewarned of an enemy approach over the broken ground on our left flank, a couple of standing patrols had been permanently assigned to the area well out in front. It was from one of these posts that three men suddenly emerged and came scurrying back. Like most men under fire, they ran half-crouched with heads down, one hand steadying a tin hat, the other grasping a rifle. It caused some amusement to watch them running for their lives across open ground, and they were greeted with a cheer when they finally dropped down safely under cover in our lines.

These men must have been ordered to close in, for when I looked round I noticed that troops in the rear were preparing to leave too. At that moment a Headquarters vehicle raced up to us and an officer in it shouted to me, 'We've got orders to pull out and make for Regima. The convoy is assembling on the track. CO wants to see you.'

So this was it; after all our defensive preparations – a withdrawal. But to be honest, it was in many ways a relief. Sceleidema was fast becoming a death trap. We were completely isolated, with no defensive wire or protecting mines, nor did we have the essential support of artillery or tanks. Yet pulling out now and forsaking our carefully planned positions to expose ourselves on open ground to the possibility of tank assault seemed hardly a better option.

Our reaction was immediate. We took little time to signal over the portees, hitch up the guns behind them, load the spare shells into an ammunition truck, gather up our personal equipment and jump aboard the vehicles. It was good to be clearing out of the danger zone. As we drove away I could see that all the old positions around Sceleidema were already deserted. The rifle companies, by this time, were milling around the track in the shelter of the escarpment where the convoy vehicles were forming up.

At the appointed rendezvous I met the other six guns and indicated where I wanted them to fan out in a semi-circle around the area where the main body of troops was gathering. The NCOs knew what to do and directed the weapons to well dispersed positions facing outwards across the open desert. Meanwhile, I drove on into the assembly area in search of battalion headquarters.

* * *

Here activity was reaching fever pitch, spurred on no doubt by the sound of enemy gunfire. Vehicles with engines racing were emerging from the cover of the numerous re-entrants of the escarpment and forming into line along the track. They were promptly set upon and boarded, pirate-style, by bands of waiting troops anxious to load up stores and equipment.

I soon located headquarters and, jumping out of my vehicle, ran up to the CO, Colonel Napier, who was in the centre of a small group. I was careful to halt smartly and salute with all the composure I could muster. He greeted me with a faint smile and casually returned my salute. I was anxious not to convey any signs of tension. He certainly showed none.

Leaning for a moment on his walking cane, he straightened up as he started to speak and drew a rough map in the sand with the point of his stick.

'Mike, I want you to take three guns well forward and try to head off any armoured vehicles that might be coming this way. Delay them as long as you can so as to give us as much time as possible to get the column under way.'

I nodded my understanding.

'The other six guns are to stay with the convoy to Regima. Good luck.'

We exchanged salutes and I was off.

As I drove back I could not help reflecting on the calm, reassuring manner in which the colonel had given me my orders. At the same time I was left with the impression that his face betrayed a feeling of discomfort. I knew that in an inescapable way he was embarrassed at the hurried retreat we were now preparing. Regardless of his being an innocent victim of the dire situation in which we now found ourselves, he was in charge and he gave the orders.

I felt sad leaving him in these circumstances. Colonel Napier was a much respected and popular commander, one who achieved results by personal example and encouragement. He was firm in his decisions but fair and always approachable. Invariably cheerful, he was a person of great charm and quick wit. He inspired men to give of their best and was the last person one would ever wish to let down.

* * *

On rejoining my company, I sent a message over to those gun commanders remaining with the column and held a short briefing for the ones coming with me. Three portees, each towing its gun, lined up in single file. A fourth vehicle, a truck carrying spare ammunition, completed the party. I jumped in beside the driver of the leading portee and our line of vehicles set off.

One could not escape a feeling of being alone and exposed as we left our own troops behind and headed south again in the direction of Sceleidema. The fort still showed signs of being besieged when it came into view over on our left. I guided our column away from the escarpment to some broken ground containing bushes and boulders which seemed to offer reasonable cover from view. From here we also had a good field of fire over the open desert on our right. I decided we would make our stand here; it was about as far forward as I thought it wise to go.

The guns were detached and moved into position while the portees and ammunition truck withdrew to some undulating ground nearby. It was impossible to hide these vehicles altogether, but this was not critical, as abandoned trucks were a common sight at times like these in the desert. With luck, if the enemy spotted them they might not immediately suspect the additional presence of three guns and their crews.

Meanwhile, we set to work burrowing in the sand, moving rocks and tearing off bushes to improve our cover and disguise the weapons. We did as much as we could in the short time available and then lay down in firing positions and waited.

Chapter 4

Survivors Escape

We were not long there before the enemy gunfire eased off, and during the brief intervals of silence that followed we heard for the first time the unmistakable and dreaded drone of distant tanks. It was like suddenly hearing the noise of traffic in a town when a pneumatic drill stops. The distance of these tanks from us was difficult to estimate; sound across a desert plain can be as deceiving as over the sea.

There was then an unexpected sound of gunfire about a mile away on our right. With the help of binoculars I recognized a battery of British two-pounders. I passed the glad tidings to the men crouching beside their weapons. It was good for morale to know that someone, somewhere, was at last fighting back, but I could not discover what they were firing at.

However, it was the tanks which we had already heard that preoccupied us. We scanned the skyline for any sign of them, but still none appeared. Instead, over to our left below the escarpment the crackle of machine guns and small arms heralded the appearance of enemy infantry. Almost as if at a given signal, the dark heads and shoulders of enemy troops rose above the crests of the foothills. At first there were only a few, but soon hundreds emerged from their hiding places and surged towards Sceleidema. They were completely exposed to us as they sprinted over the rough ground and stormed the area of the fort. Meeting no resistance, the assault troops just scrambled over the place for a while and then regrouped. They proceeded cautiously along the foot of the escarpment in pursuit of our troops who had now withdrawn. Those leading the advance went to ground from time to time and appeared to be exchanging fire with a Welch rearguard.

My men had been spectators of all this and some were tempted with the idea of using their rifles on what seemed easy targets, but I scotched any such notions. No doubt we could have inflicted some casualties, but at the risk of drawing attention to ourselves. So far our presence had gone unnoticed, and it was imperative to keep it that way.

Increasing numbers of enemy soldiers joined in the advance along the foot of the escarpment, and in their wake came light vehicles and ambulances. If they continued on their present line of march they would bypass us and we would escape their attention altogether. These were comforting thoughts but, alas, they were soon shattered.

Away on the skyline immediately to our front, another formation of enemy troops had suddenly appeared and was coming our way. They were some distance off, however, and unlikely to discover us for a while yet; but it made me wonder how much longer we could risk remaining where we were. I had no communication with battalion HQ so was ignorant about events or intentions elsewhere.

There were certainly enemy tanks in the vicinity preparing to go into action, but there was nothing we could do about it unless they presented themselves.

With the passing of every minute the closer the oncoming infantry would be to our position and the greater would be the danger of being overrun and losing our guns. If and when we did make a move, it would be in full view of the enemy, and the longer we delayed it, the more vulnerable we should be to their fire. I was turning these problems over in my mind, trying to come to a decision, when, quite unexpectedly, the decision was made for me.

A light truck was sighted to our rear speeding over the open ground towards our parked vehicles. These vehicles, no doubt, had been seen by the enemy before this, even though they had not spotted us or our low-lying guns. They would have assumed such vehicles to be abandoned transport – not an uncommon sight – and have counted on collecting them after the battle. Capturing material is preferable to destroying it.

The enemy, too, must have witnessed the approach of this lone vehicle and, sensing something was afoot, started firing mortar shells into the area. We kept our heads down and awaited the arrival of the visitor.

The car stopped by our parked vehicles and one of the drivers directed it to where I was lying. It was OC Headquarter Company, and as he drew near he leaned out of the window and shouted, 'I've been looking for you buggers everywhere! CO wants you back straight away!' I indicated acknowledgement while the car swerved round and disappeared in a cloud of dust.

Orders were superfluous; in a flash, the men were on their feet and calling over the vehicles. Engines were started and guns dragged out from their cover to be hooked behind portees, while ammunition boxes and rifles were slung up onto the open trucks. Finally the crews scrambled aboard to begin the race back.

Two portees and guns got clean away immediately without incident, but the third portee was showing no signs of life. Its engine could not be started. A dent in its bonnet from a mortar was possibly the cause. Try as we might, we could get no response from it. But worse was to follow, for at that same moment we spotted a contingent of about fifty enemy infantry detaching themselves from those near the escarpment and heading our way. We should have to move quickly.

By good fortune our small reserve ammunition truck had not yet got under way; it was now our only hope. Frantically we signalled it over to the immobile portee and secured a steel rope between them. The strain was taken up, and after a few jerks our little procession started to move. As it gathered speed I jumped on, thankful to have got everyone away safely, including the last gun.

Private Jones took the wheel of the portee which, although damaged, could still be steered. I was alongside him while Corporal Shaw sat in the back keeping an eye on the trailing gun bouncing madly over the rough ground. The two other members of the gun crew were riding in the back of the ammunition truck towing us.

It was no light task for this small truck, already loaded itself, to drag behind a disabled portee plus gun. However, the going was firm and we made good headway, keeping well clear of the escarpment to avoid any small arms fire that might be directed at us from the leading enemy troops. These we soon overtook and pressed on, expecting to catch up with our own unit which could not be far off now. But we were due for a surprise.

* * *

The solid surface we had been driving over suddenly gave way to softer, deeper sand, causing our ammunition truck to slip, flounder and lose speed.

Our preoccupation with this and the enemy on our right had, for the moment, left us oblivious to events developing elsewhere. The fact was that over the horizon, across the plain to our left rear, enemy tanks had finally emerged. They were approaching in full view.

These monsters created a shelf of dust as they charged over the flat wastes, while their tracks sent up waves of sand like the wash of speedboats. They were going at full speed, travelling due north in two long columns. They were on a course roughly parallel to our own but, as far as I could judge, did not, for the moment, appear to be closing in on us.

This caused me to wonder if they were intent on reaching some important objective like Benghazi, while ignoring relatively small targets such as ourselves. But this proved to be wishful thinking! As they drew abreast, one column peeled off, making a half right turn, and advanced on the escarpment well ahead of us. The intention, it seemed, was to cut off the retreat of the Welch.

Having approached to within a few hundred yards of their target, the enemy tanks halted and their assault began in earnest. They fired at point blank range on troops and transport trapped beneath the escarpment. The result of this one-sided contest was soon apparent in the burning wreckage of our exposed and vulnerable vehicles. I wondered what part our other anti-tank guns in front were playing in this exchange of fire. The tanks themselves were shrouded in dust and smoke as streaks of fire continued to pour from them towards the Welch positions. Above it all, the repetitive bark of their cannons echoed through the hills.

Meanwhile, we struggled on, our portee bumping and lurching clumsily as it was dragged reluctantly over the uneven ground. We were clear of enemy troops on our right, but the arrival of hostile tanks on our left posed a new and serious threat, a threat that was soon a reality.

A screeching shell and an explosion, perilously near us, was a warning that we ourselves were now drawing the fire of one or more tanks. Our leading driver instinctively veered towards the escarpment, where the foothills might offer some hope of sanctuary. But there was no cover immediately in sight, and at the speed we were travelling there was little prospect of our ever reaching there anyway. With tanks now harassing us we were virtually trapped.

The immediate danger was the possibility of the ammunition truck receiving a direct hit; that would certainly be the end of us all. Then a second explosion on nearby rocks shook us and the vehicles. Flying shrapnel must have sprayed the two men peering over the tailboard of the ammunition truck towing us, as their haunted faces were suddenly covered in blood. I decided to act.

Right now we were on a suicide course and sooner or later we would fall victim to the deadly cannon of the tank engaging us. By detaching ourselves from the ammunition truck and relieving it of its burden, it might make the safety of the hills; at the same time, having dismounted, we could bring our gun into action on the hostile tank. With a broken-down portee we should, of course, be stranded, but it seemed the only course of action.

I yelled at the injured men in the front truck to warn their driver to halt. Just at that moment, a shell passed between the truck and our portee, grazing the taut steel towing wire and causing it to vibrate like the plucked string of a double bass. The driver got the message and stopped, enabling us to jump out and detach our portee. Thus relieved of its burden, the ammunition truck catapulted off with a new lease of life.

Meanwhile, the three of us unhooked the gun from its stricken portee, grabbed a couple of boxes of ammunition and dragged them to some broken ground near the foot of the ridge. We swung it into position, pointing its muzzle at the enemy and took up our familiar stations around it.

Corporal Shaw crouched down ready to aim and fire and Private Jones knelt behind the protective shield waiting to load a shell into the breach, while I lay to one side prepared to direct the fire. Our target was obvious, a lone tank in an advanced position, sitting out there with its gun menacing us.

Shaw seized the lever to open the breech prior to loading but could not move it. He struggled frantically with it, but to no effect. Another shell streaked past and buried itself silently in the dunes behind us. Jones was up in a flash to help. He, too, tugged at the lever, but to no effect. He yelled over to me, 'It's been damaged!' I crawled over to see for myself and, on a closer look at the breech mechanism, realized there was little chance of getting it open. Vainly we wrestled with the lever in a last desperate effort to move it, but it was useless. Another near miss from the tank caused us to sprawl in the sand. We seemed doomed.

In this hopeless situation we could only take cover, but if we remained where we were we would be in danger of capture by enemy infantrymen steadily advancing along the base of the ridge who could not be very far off. There was only one way out of our dilemma, and that was to climb the escarpment behind us.

Simultaneously we jumped to our feet and started scrambling up the slopes as fast as we could. But if we thought we had shaken off the attentions of the tank we were mistaken. As soon as we exposed ourselves, it directed its cannon on us again. It had no intention of letting us escape in this way.

We were not encumbered by hand weapons, which were still in the abandoned portee out on the plain, so we were able to move swiftly. Climbing was less difficult than it had seemed from the ground, but occasionally we had to zigzag to tackle the steeper parts.

The tank gave us no respite and shells continued to thud into the ground around us – it was like using a sledge hammer to crack a nut. Needless to say, all this spurred us on as we mounted the escarpment, scurrying and scrambling like hunted animals.

Before long we were well above the battlefield, and to our great relief the tank ceased firing at us. Perhaps the cannon had reached its maximum elevation. We did not relax, however, until about half way up I hit upon a ledge and flung myself down on it. I was ahead of the other two, and it was some seconds later before they appeared and dropped down beside me. We lay there for a while panting and gasping for breath. It was the first occasion for several hours that day that we had been free from hostile shelling and shooting, a welcome moment of peace for which I gave a prayer of thanks.

We glanced at each other with faint smiles, sharing the joy of deliverance. Jones was the first to speak. Giggling to himself and in an excited voice he stammered, 'You should have seen one of those bloody shells, Sir! Missed your foot by inches! Buried itself in the sand just as you jumped clear!' Then he burst out laughing.

From our elevated position on the ledge we had a bird's eye view of the whole scene. On the left we could observe the enemy advancing in depth, with reserves of men and materials following up. To our front, their tanks and mobile columns on the plain were disengaging themselves from the action and moving northwards again. Immediately to our right front, where the main battle had taken place, and now partly hidden by high ground, the enemy forces were presumably mopping up. That area was still engulfed in fumes and tall pillars of black smoke were curling skywards in the still evening air. Only sporadic firing could now be heard above the drone of moving enemy transport.

Some 300ft below we spotted an enemy open-tracked vehicle resting at the bottom of a narrow trail winding up the escarpment. There were half a dozen soldiers sitting in the back and an officer was standing beside the vehicle was looking through binoculars clearly trained on us. In return, I did the same with my glasses. The officer promptly alighted and pointed up the track; the carrier started to climb. No doubt they were searching for stragglers like ourselves. We decided it was time to be off and resumed the ascent.

As we continued our way up I kept an eye on this vehicle. But we had no need to worry. Very soon it ran into difficulties and started slipping back. Its tracks turned furiously trying to get a grip, but finally it gave up the struggle and, much to our delight, turned around and descended.

We were now confident of having evaded the enemy altogether and resumed the climb with lighter hearts. Another ten minutes and the three of us reached the top and safety.

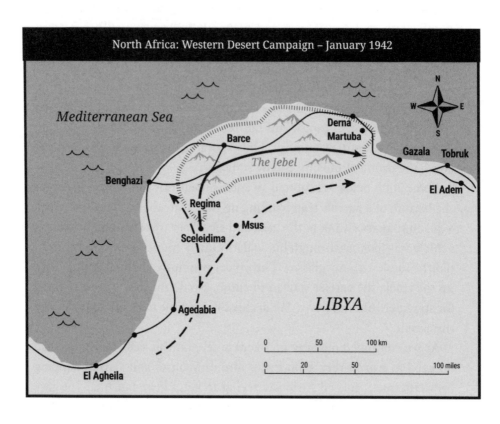

North Africa: Western Desert Campaign – January 1942

Mediterranean Sea

Derna
Martuba
Barce
The Jebel
Gazala
Tobruk
Benghazi
El Adem
Regima
Msus
Sceleidima

LIBYA

0   50   100 km

0   20   50   100 miles

Agedabia

El Agheila

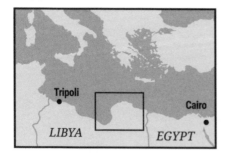

Mediterranean Area

Tripoli
Cairo
LIBYA
EGYPT

Italian - German Attack – – – –

Welch Party Withdrawal ——————

Chapter 5

Forced Night March

On top of the escarpment there was complete silence; it seemed another world. Down below the fury of the battle had abated. Those of our troops who had not managed to get away must now have been overrun. Perhaps some of our transport had evaded the guns of the enemy tanks and escaped northwards. For those of us left behind and still free, the next move was clear. Orders were to make for Regima, a town some 50 miles north.

If the columns which had passed Sceleidema today had the intention of veering north-west and converging on the all-important town of Benghazi with its vital port, then Regima, due north of us, might still be ours. On the other hand, if the 4th Indian Division, of which the Welch were part, had been ordered to withdraw from these parts altogether, then Regima, along with Benghazi, might have been evacuated. Whatever was happening, if we were to have any chance of catching up with our own troops we would have to move quickly.

The crescent-shaped region of the Jebel Akhdar (green mountain), on which we now found ourselves, reached north and then east, following the curve of the Cyrenaican coastline for 200 miles. This limestone tableland, covered with *maquis* and woods and cut by ravines and caves, contrasted with the endless sands and desolation around it. It was the homeland of Senussi Arab nomads who wandered around seeking fertile areas for their small herds of sheep and goats. It had also been the last stronghold of these tribesmen resisting the invading Italian forces of Graziani before their surrender ten years earlier. Their fighting spirit, however, had not been broken. They still managed to carry arms, and a voluntary contingent was at that moment serving with the Eighth Army. We had reason to believe, therefore, that when meeting up with these people, as we were bound to, we should find them friendly.

* * *

We were not alone high up on the escarpment, for a few other British and Indian soldiers had, like ourselves, escaped the clutches of the enemy by scaling the heights. All looked weary and subdued. A few were nursing minor wounds; some colleagues, they said, who had been more seriously injured, had been picked up quickly by an Italian ambulance advancing with the forward troops. The morale of all these men had been undermined by the day's humiliations, and I sensed some resentment, especially from those men not of my regiment, when I ordered them all to gather round for a briefing on what was to be done.

I tried to rally their spirits by addressing them in what I hoped was a firm voice and confident manner. I repeated our last order, which was to close on Regima. It would mean a forced march over 50 miles or so and, provided the going was good, we should make it in twelve hours. I stressed the importance of covering as much ground as possible during the hours of darkness so as to minimize the dangers tomorrow of moving when it was light. As a final spur, I warned them that if we were spotted and attacked by enemy armoured patrols, they would be unlikely, in those parts, to burden themselves with prisoners.

The sun was setting and the short desert twilight was giving way to a cloudless night. We set off in the fading light.

* * *

With the help of a map and compass, I set a course and led the way. Conditions were ideal; the night air was cool, while a pale half moon gave just sufficient light to assist in keeping our bearings. It was stony and rough underfoot but there were no major obstacles, it seemed, and we were able to follow a fairly direct route at a fast pace. Speed was essential.

The group seemed in good heart and the first few hours went well. Gradually, however, as time passed, stragglers began to fall behind. Although all were young and well used to physical hardships, the shock and strain of the day's events, combined with growing thirst, were having an effect. I had already abandoned the Army regulation ten-minute halt every hour on the march and substituted a five-minute break every half hour. It was the only way to keep everyone together.

Some men had rifles – a heavy burden on a forced march – which I arranged to change round at each halt so we could all share in the task of carrying them. I may have been wrong, but at one of these changeovers I had the strongest suspicion that one or more of these weapons had been quietly discarded en route.

Some men had voiced dissension at the idea of proceeding to Regima and were in favour of striking due east out of the battle area altogether. I scotched this plan, insisting that we had our orders and that if it proved impossible to carry them out, then and only then would we take matters into our own hands.

For all my brave words I confess I had misgivings about Regima. I was hoping beyond hope that we would meet up with our own troops there as planned, but considering the vast distances already covered by Rommel in his lightning offensive, and having seen his armoured columns today running free and virtually unopposed, the prospect of arresting the onslaught in these parts did not seem good to me.

But then about midnight came the heartening sounds of gunfire from the direction of Benghazi. That could mean only one thing – its defenders were resisting. If Benghazi was holding out, it was most likely that Regima was still in our hands. However, within an hour or so, the gunfire ceased, so once more we were left in doubt.

We maintained our forced march through the night, and when the light of dawn crept up, it revealed a very different scene from the one we had left behind on the previous day. The barrenness of the desert with its grey sands and stones was no more. Instead, we found ourselves surrounded by stretches of grass, clumps of bushes and even trees. We also discovered an occasional muddy patch containing pools of water, from which we were glad to slake our thirsts. I calculated that during darkness we had covered about 35 miles and that provided we had kept on course, we should be some 15 miles from our objective, Regima.

It was not long before we met our first local inhabitant – a shepherd sitting cross-legged on the ground wrapped in an army blanket. His animals withdrew to a safe distance as we approached. We pressed him with questions about the enemy but communication was difficult. He regarded us suspiciously and pleaded ignorance of everything. However, at the sound of the name Regima he tilted his head backwards and pointed a bearded chin in the direction we were going. Glad of this confirmation, we thanked him and resumed our march. He did not bother to look up.

In due course we hit upon a trail which, according to our compass, was converging on our objective, Regima. But trails are a sign of life, so caution was called for. However, with the growing prospect of reaching journey's end, and despite fatigue, the pace of the men noticeably quickened.

Towards midday, when crossing some high ground, we sighted a town a few miles away which we reckoned was Regima. We halted for a moment while I used my binoculars. Suddenly we were surprised by a group of young Arabs. They had emerged through bushes from an encampment nearby, well hidden by scrub. They had obviously spotted us long before we had seen them. Nomads were adept at concealing their temporary dwelling places – a practice long since adopted as a precaution against would-be marauders.

These young men, most of whom were carrying firearms, showed no fear. I suspect they recognized us for what we were. They proved friendly and talkative and eagerly accepted cigarettes, which were passed around.

Soon the company was laughing and joking, with remarks from our men like, 'Tell your sister to come here.' For a brief moment the war was forgotten. The happy atmosphere quickly changed, however, when our friends, after confirming the place in sight was, indeed, Regima, also assured us that the British had left.

This was bad news, if true. I was downcast and avoided catching the eyes of the others. One slumped to the ground cursing and spitting in disgust. A few argued that we should not rely too much on this evidence, but most of us felt our informants would have no reason to lie. Anyway, being within sight of the place, we should soon find out for ourselves. The march was resumed in a sombre mood.

As we drew nearer to Regima, traffic could be seen moving out of the town along the road running eastwards. Peering through my field glasses I could hardly believe my eyes. What I saw were unmistakably British vehicles – our familiar 3-ton lorries – but before I had time to rejoice I saw something else too – a convoy of Axis vehicles. Our 3-tonners were clearly newly captured transport put to immediate use by the enemy – a common practice. Now there could be no more doubt, Regima had fallen. We were too late, our forced march had been in vain.

Naturally, we were disappointed, but not really surprised. We had, more or less, resigned ourselves to this possibility, but at least the position was clear and we knew what was to be done. For our part, we had carried out our orders as far as we had been able; now there would be no more orders.

* * *

It was a strange new feeling to be suddenly free of all authority. I cannot deny experiencing a mild sensation of exhilaration – the kind a schoolboy knows when playing truant beyond the reach of his masters. Now the onus was entirely on us. We had to brace ourselves for the prospect of a long, hazardous journey on foot to outwit the enemy and reach the safety of our own lines. It was an exciting challenge.

Taking a last look at Regima, the place seemed quiet; there were no signs of hostilities, and further back still in the direction of Benghazi there was only silence too. Everything pointed to the Eighth Army having pulled out of this corner of Cyrenaica completely during the night. There being neither sound nor sight of a front, we could only conclude that it had moved a considerable distance from where we now found ourselves. Some local Arabs passing by at that moment asserted that the nearest Allied troops were at Gazala. This seemed far back, but the speed of Rommel's latest advance led us to believe that it could well be true. Short, therefore, of an unlikely sudden reversal of fortune, we had to face the likelihood of a walk of perhaps 150 miles.

I turned to the men and discussed the problems and prospects of the long trek ahead. I reminded them that we were now deep into the enemy's rear areas, where he would be thin on the ground and consequently there would be less danger of our discovery; also that the Jebel Akhdar terrain over which we would be moving offered good cover from view and that the local Senussi Arabs, who would be our only hope of obtaining food, appeared friendly enough. I warned them to be always on guard, however, and to keep off roads and avoid settlements. I advised them, when nearing the front, to make for the southern flank, where troop concentrations would be less heavy. There was not much more to be said, and the men seemed subdued and engaged in their own thoughts.

Our group numbered eighteen, far too many to keep together in this situation; besides, there were very few arms between us. So as a first step I picked out the six fittest men, not of my own regiment, and sent them on their way under command of an RASC sergeant. The rest of us, mostly Welch and including two Indian soldiers, remained behind for the time being.

It was the hottest time of the day. We dropped down under what shade we could find, relieved our weary feet of boots, then lay back and relaxed in the luxury of a much needed period of undisturbed rest. We had been on the move for twenty-four hours and sleep had finally caught up with us.

Chapter 6

All Contact Lost

After a few hours' refreshing sleep, we made preparations to resume the march. There was much groaning as sore feet were eased into hard Army boots, but finally everyone dragged himself up ready to move on. It was a jaded band of men that shuffled along a stony track at the commencement of what promised to be a long walk home. We were all a bit hungry, too, and not knowing where our next meal would come from seemed to make it worse. However, we had a little money between us and hoped to be able to beg or buy food on the way.

The afternoon's march was uneventful and we encountered no one. We kept well out of sight of the main east-west road, leaving Regima well behind us. Before dark we were fortunate to come across an Arab encampment, where we managed to obtain some pancake-like loaves of bread.

After nightfall we halted to rest, but sleep for any long period was not possible because of the cold. Lying on the ground without blankets, one soon started shivering. We therefore plodded on for another half hour or so until we felt warm enough to take another rest. This was repeated throughout the night, until the comforting glow of the sun's rays the following morning enabled us to have a couple of hours' unbroken sleep.

Early next day, we were heartened by what sounded like distant gunfire, which could indicate that we were not entirely out of contact with the front. It must have helped rally spirits, for the pace noticeably increased and we made very good progress. Even so, it was becoming increasingly obvious that some men were feeling the strain of forced marching. Prior to our entry into the desert operations we had undergone a period of hard training in the Nile Delta at a camp called Beni Usif, within sight of the Great Pyramids of Giza. Repeated day-long marches and exercises had toughened and prepared us for the forthcoming campaign. However, the nature of modern desert warfare was such that, since leaving the base, we had spent more time in and out of vehicles than foot-slogging. Now we were paying for it!

Some men were anxious to push on at a faster rate. They would get well ahead and then rest while the others caught up. It seemed unfair to hold them back in this way, and in any case there was no virtue in keeping the group together any longer. On the contrary, there were very sound reasons for splitting it up. We were dependent on the goodwill of the Arabs for food, and since they were difficult to locate and usually poor, they could not be expected to offer hospitality to a large body of hungry men like ourselves.

I put this point to the men, stressing that their chances of making it back to the lines would be improved by our separating into smaller groups and moving independently. Additionally, concealment from the enemy would be easier, and this would become increasingly important as we approached the front. All were agreed, and it was decided that on the following day we should split up into twos and threes.

* * *

The next morning at first light we came across an isolated cluster of buildings – an Italian colonial settlement. There was no sign of life. Just then a solitary shepherd with a couple of animals passed us, so we stopped him and enquired about this place. We used the two Indian soldiers for these occasions; they seemed able to communicate with the Arabs more easily than we could.

We gathered that British soldiers had been living there but two days ago they had left, and now the place was empty. We decided to investigate.

On drawing closer we found the doors and shutters open. I gave a warning about booby traps and then we entered silently. But there was nothing to fear, the place was deserted. It was a typical farmstead with an inner courtyard and outbuildings. The exterior pink walls were spattered with bullet holes but the building was undamaged. The interior had been stripped of its contents, apart from some heavy furniture, including a long dining table and Tudor-style leather-covered chairs. The floors were beautifully laid with patterned marble tiles, suggesting a once grand residence. The kitchen was littered with empty tins and utensils; the only sign of cooking was in the courtyard.

Suddenly there were shouts of delight from one of the outhouses, and Corporal Shaw appeared at a doorway holding an unopened crate of our own familiar 'bully beef' – a wonderful discovery. This spurred on the others in the search for more food, and it was not long before someone else ferreted out a good-sized tin of what proved to be tomato purée. It was not the first time I had witnessed the look of disgust on the face of a soldier on opening a tin from captured enemy stores to find it contained just this, when he had been hoping for jam. Tomato purée may have been an essential ingredient of the Italian soldier's fare but it had no place in the artless cooking of the British Tommy!

We were all anxious for hot food again, having been without it for so long. Now was our chance, and in no time the corned beef was opened up, tipped into a container of fresh water and brought to the boil over a wood-fired stove. I had suggested flavouring it with the tomato purée but this was turned down. Hungry faces gazed expectantly at the steaming pot until it was ready. Then it was a jovial company indeed that sat down to enjoy the feast. There was plenty of meat and hot broth to go round, but with our boundless appetites nothing was left. The story in the scriptures of manna from heaven falling in the desert passed through my mind.

I did not think it wise to tarry too long at this place. I had taken the precaution of posting a couple of lookouts, and although we were not on a main through road, it was best to take no chances as our presence was already known to a local shepherd.

Before leaving, and after a short briefing, our unwieldy band of twelve was split up, as agreed, into five parties of two and three. I then despatched them at suitable intervals, the fittest going first. Each group was provided with a rough sketch map of the area taken from my Ordnance Survey map and armed with at least one rifle. I was the last to leave, accompanied by Corporal Shaw and Private Jones. The latter was already a lame duck and the slowest mover of us all.

I was not sorry to see the back of some of the grousers, but I missed the company of the humorists. In times of stress they are the ones who help relieve tension and boost morale. Baden-Powell, the founder of the scout movement, was right, I think, to place so much emphasis on the importance of cheerfulness in human relations. For my part, I had no doubt that some of the men were pleased to have shaken off the authority of an officer and be left to their own devices. But Corporal Shaw and Private Jones regarded it as quite natural to remain with me. They were the only ones of my original company, and we knew each other well by this time.

Having eaten handsomely at the start of the day, we were not bothered by our stomachs and were able to concentrate on getting on, so made steady progress. In the early afternoon, with the sun at its hottest, we were taking a rest when we heard voices approaching. We peered out from behind the bushes under which we were sheltering and recognized British uniforms. It was a group of Indian soldiers. We hailed them and exchanged greetings. They were from a unit of the 4th Indian Division that had been trapped near Benghazi by Rommel's two-pronged thrust from Msus. Most of the division had extricated itself, but their unit had been overrun and most of them taken prisoner. However, that same night, these few managed to slip their guards and steal away under cover of darkness. They were in very good spirits and clearly elated at having redeemed themselves from the shame of surrender.

They seemed already well adjusted to their situation. Food was no problem; they had purchased a sheep from the Senussi, slaughtered it in accordance with their religious rites and consumed it. Even now, they were carrying a plentiful supply of Arab-made chapatis. In these surroundings they must have felt more at home than we did.

They were in a hurry to be off, and after pressing some of their precious chapatis on us they saluted, turned on their heels and were gone.

One could not fail to admire the Indian soldier. He was in every sense the perfect professional. Coming from far-off Asia, he could surely not be motivated to risk his life the way we were; his home and family were not threatened by the Germans. Yet his devotion to duty was equal to ours. Two of the platoons in my anti-tank company were from Indian regiments, and their bearing, standard of turnout and discipline were exemplary.

* * *

Our pace had considerably slackened since that first day's burst of 50 miles in fifteen hours. Now, after another morning's march, we had hardly achieved five, but this was due to poor Jones, whose blisters were crippling him and on top of which he was feverish.

We had come about 60 miles from Regima and reckoned we were now somewhere south of Barce, the next nearest large town on our line of march through the Jebel Akhdar. We met some local inhabitants and asked the usual questions about the war situation. To our surprise, they claimed that Barce was still held by the British. This seemed most unlikely to us. Anyway, we decided it was worth investigating and so turned off northwards.

Barce was near the heart of the Jebel Akhdar region. This area was ideal guerrilla country but unsuitable for tanks and mobile warfare. Commanders on both sides had never committed themselves to its defence for very long; they preferred to get off it and down into the desert plains where there was room for manoeuvre. It contained some airfields, but otherwise troops confined themselves to the few towns and main roads. Because of this, we were able to move freely around the surrounding countryside with relative safety.

By mid-afternoon Jones was feeling much worse, and it was clear that, at the speed we were walking, we would not get within sight of Barce that day as it was still several miles distant. I decided, therefore, to go on alone and told Jones to rest where he was until I returned. Leaving Corporal Shaw with him, I pushed on as fast as I could.

It took considerably longer to reach Barce than I had expected – two hours. As I approached I stopped from time to time to make observations through my field glasses since I could detect much movement. Finally the truth became apparent; the activity was a parade of Axis vehicles draped in flags, while the buildings around were festooned in Italian tricolours. The populace were celebrating the re-entry of Axis forces. Once again we had been foiled. I had half expected it anyway, but I was sorry to have to give this news to Shaw and Jones. I wasted no time in starting back.

An hour later the light began to fade under a heavily overcast sky which threatened a change in the weather. I quickened my pace, but it was not long before large drops of rain started to fall while it grew noticeably darker. Suddenly the storm broke with a mighty clap of thunder and lightning. I had just passed a stone hut and I raced back to it for shelter.

It was dry inside and its sole occupant was a small white dog – fortunately friendly. I stood at the open doorway watching the torrential rain outside and resigned myself to the fact that I would not make it back to Shaw and Jones that evening.

Later on, I lay down on the floor listening to the rain pounding the roof while the little dog curled up beside me. It was bitterly cold and I was glad of the added warmth of his shivering body.

By first light the sky had cleared and I raised myself up feeling stiff and damp. My little companion had already departed, and I set out myself, estimating that there would still be a good hour's march back to my starting point.

The last stages of this return journey were proving increasingly difficult. More than once the track I had been following split into two, and in this wilderness of shrubs and bushes, with no prominent features for guidance, I could only hope I had chosen the right path. There had been no problem on the journey out as all paths seemed to converge on the town like the spokes of a wheel. But now, in the reverse direction, not even my compass was of much help.

As I approached, I hoped, the place where I had left my colleagues, I kept a sharp lookout for any signs of life, but there was no one to be seen anywhere. I searched the surrounding area for a while but it proved fruitless. Perhaps they had decided to move on when I failed to show up yesterday, or they may have sought shelter somewhere during the night's storm; I myself may have drifted off course. Many possibilities existed, but the plain fact was that I had lost them and was now alone.

Chapter 7

Life (and Near Death) with the Arabs

I continued my journey eastwards, moving parallel to the main Barce–Derna road. On my own, concealment was easier, and I was able to stay close enough to the road to keep it under observation for much of the time. My rate of progress had also speeded up. Time, however, was inevitably lost endeavouring to secure food. The only source was the local inhabitants, as nothing edible grew at this time of the year. Fortunately, the Senussi Arabs proved to be extremely hospitable, ever ready to share their food with a stranger.

The main difficulty, voyaging through unfamiliar country, was locating the Senussi. They were thin on the ground and invariably pitched their tents in well-concealed places, astutely hidden or camouflaged by mounds and bushes. It was not easy to spot them from a distance and, more often than not, one stumbled upon them without warning. Oddly enough, I found it easier to locate them at night than by day. This was because their dogs, which were usually quiet during the day, seemed to find their voices after dark to give warning of the approach of strangers. I was often assisted in 'homing in' on an encampment by this means.

One such occasion was during my fourth night out on my own. I was very hungry, not having eaten for twenty-four hours. Then from somewhere to my front came the distant, welcome barking of a dog. Naturally cheered at the prospect of at last obtaining food, I veered off in the direction of the likely encampment, but after a few minutes the barking stopped. All I could do now was to press on, hoping to keep on course.

Suddenly and without warning a dog sprang out of the bushes and attacked me. I lashed out with my boot. It withdrew out of reach and then set up a prolonged howling and barking. As long as I remained still, it did not threaten me, but each time I started to move it came for me again.

Finding myself pinned down by this vicious animal, I knelt down and groped around for a large stone but could find nothing.

I crouched there on the ground feeling helpless and rather foolish. It was a pale moonlit night, and I became aware, suddenly, of the presence of a dark hooded figure silhouetted above a mound a few yards away. It had crept up on me in complete silence. Startled, I jumped to my feet, but at that moment the stranger must have spotted me, for in a single movement a rifle was swung from his shoulder, pointed at me and fired. Instinctively I dropped to the ground and yelled 'Ingleesh!' The shot missed but it must have been close; I had clearly seen the flash from the muzzle.

The lone figure hesitated a moment but did not fire a second time. With the rifle still pointing at me he called the dog behind him and beckoned me to come forward. I got up and as I came closer I could see the bearded features of an Arab beneath the hood. He took a long hard look at me then slung his weapon back on his shoulder and without uttering a word signalled me to follow. The dog, now pacified, trotted happily behind.

We descended a hill and arrived at an encampment of two or three tents. He led me into one of them. There was a woman inside, presumably his wife, but she was promptly dismissed. He invited me to sit down, and using sign language, asked if I were hungry. I indicated that I was. He shouted something to his wife, who must have been waiting outside. Shortly afterwards, she came back in bearing a shallow dish containing a porridge-like mixture. It was hot, sweet and stodgy – just what I needed; gratefully I ate it all.

It was then suggested that I should sleep there. I needed no persuasion, and removing my boots, I crawled into the bedding already spread on the floor. My host joined me, and after extinguishing the oil lamp, pulled a large straw matting over us both. It was warm and dry and I settled down to enjoy my most comfortable night since leaving Sceleidima. I slept in peace with my would-be assassin.

* * *

Apart from such occasional contact with strangers, I had been for the greater part of four days quite alone. I suppose complete solitude for this length of time is something few people have experienced. I think it was the first time in my life for me. It started to depress me, and I had moments of painful homesickness. It was only by keeping on the move that I succeeded in shaking off this melancholia.

I could, of course, count myself lucky that the Senussis regarded the British as allies helping to liberate their country. Their long and bitter struggle with the Italians was still fresh in their minds. Although they were by nature generous and hospitable, I doubt whether an Axis soldier in my predicament, and there must have been many from time to time, would have found them so charitably disposed. Most Senussis carried firearms and spoke of revenge.

* * *

In the early hours of the next day, under cover of pouring rain, I crossed the main road to have a look at the small airfield at Maraua. My unit had lagered there one night during the Allied advance. As far as I could see through the mist, there were no signs of the enemy using it yet. All that was visible were a few sabotaged enemy aircraft on the perimeter, relics of the work of our Long Range Desert Group several months before.

I recrossed the road and after I had sheltered a while, the sun broke through, enabling me to press on and cover some 15 miles during daylight.

* * *

That evening, I encountered a tall young shepherd tending the largest flock of sheep that I had seen in these parts. He had been grazing them and was on the point of driving them home when we met. It needed only a few words of introduction for him to size up my situation and invite me to accompany him. We walked for a long way, and it was almost dark by the time we arrived at his destination, a fairly large encampment.

His tent was a new one and, judging by the rather superior furnishings inside, he was obviously wealthy by local standards. His wife, too, was young and attractive and dressed in gay colours, unlike most of the Senussi women who were clothed in dowdy garments, often in rags.

After a long day alone in the damp and cold it felt good to sit with company before a charcoal fire in such a cosy home. There was the usual procession of male members of the tribe entering the tent, curious to see me and exchange words of greeting. Food was soon forthcoming, consisting of the now familiar porridge-like fare in a shallow dish placed on the floor. We sat round it cross-legged and in turn scooped it up with four fingers until it was finished.

After the meal I made preparations to leave, but the young couple insisted on my staying the night; it was raining heavily. The wife produced blankets for me and then took her leave. Before long I was curled up, warm, contented and snug, listening to the rain pounding on the roof of the tent.

* * *

The morning skies were clear once more as I set out. How refreshed one felt after sleeping comfortably all night. I had been lucky to find lodgings for two nights like this. Indeed, one could sometimes pass a whole day without seeing a sign of habitation. Occasionally one might cross paths with a nomad family on the move. Their camel or donkey would be loaded with their tent and belongings, while the children trailed behind, herding a few sheep and goats. Usually they took no notice of me and hurried on in silence. But that day, by contrast, I was to discover a whole Senussi village where I was made welcome and treated to traditional Arab hospitality.

I might have missed it altogether had not some children appeared, seemingly from nowhere, and surrounded me. I was led through the bush and emerged in a clearing where there were tents pitched all round. I was hesitant about entering a strange place of this size, but the noisy reception of the children roused others and I found myself escorted through the village towards the tent of one whom I assumed must be the headman.

Inside, I was given a very warm welcome from the elders of the community with handshakes all round. We sat around a charcoal fire attempting to communicate. I endeavoured to put a brave face on the recent misfortunes of the Eighth Army by describing the tremendous build-up of arms in Egypt and how the enemy would soon be driven from their land altogether. It was all in my imagination, of course, but it seemed to impress them; or were they perhaps simply being polite? For their part, they gave me what I considered to be a reliable military situation report. Derna had been taken, they said, but the Axis forces had been halted in the Gazala area. This seemed realistic to me, and I calculated that provided the front stabilized there, I had a good chance of being back on our own side within three days.

I prepared to leave, but it was suggested that I first join them for tea. It was a ritual I had experienced before and I knew it would delay me another half hour at least. I was keen to be off but I also realized it would have been impolite to refuse. So the customary polished casket was produced, containing six small silver cups and a metal teapot. In due course the tea was made and handed carefully around.

Tea was highly prized but it was scarce and expensive, so for these poor nomads it was a great luxury. It was common to see Arab boys on the roadside bartering fresh eggs for tea with passing army convoys. My men had often done such deals. I recalled now with satisfaction how I had reprimanded a soldier, much to his surprise, when he boasted of having passed off used and dried tea leaves in an exchange. Generally speaking, there was little understanding or sympathy for the Arabs among the military. In the desert there was rarely any contact anyway, but back in the crowded streets of Cairo one frequently witnessed off-duty soldiers taking pleasure in cursing and ridiculing local Egyptians. Although most units were well disciplined out of barracks, instances of this sort must have given us all a bad name and we were probably despised for it.

While we were taking tea under an open tent, a small crowd of chattering women and children had gathered outside to watch the proceedings at a respectable distance. Women always seemed to be relegated to the role of spectator on social occasions. However, they were quick to join in the merriment and excitement which broke out when the chief called for a certain infant boy to be brought over. I failed to understand the reason for all this until the chief proudly presented him to me as an Australian. I patted the child on the head which brought another round of laughter, and the party broke up on a high note. The chief then bade me farewell and insisted on providing an armed escort to the top of the next hill, from which vantage point my best line of march would be shown me.

The two youths who accompanied me out of the village were curious to know if I was armed. I had often been asked this by youngsters but never by older men, possibly out of politeness, as it seemed to be a matter of prestige. Although I had long since been parted from my pistol and holster, left in the stricken portee at Sceleidima, I invariably gave my enquirers a knowing look and pointed inside my battledress blouse. This always worked.

* * *

The weather for the next two days was clear and dry and I made the most of it by keeping on the move and resisting the temptation to deviate for the purpose of finding food. I covered perhaps 40 miles and finally, at evening, got my reward – the sound of gunfire. I knew at long last I was in touch with the front.

That same evening, thanks to the barking of dogs, I located an encampment where I received food and shelter. After two nights out I was glad of the chance of an unbroken night's sleep, which only the comfort and warmth of a bed can give. On this occasion I was to have the company of half a dozen newborn goats.

They were brought into the tent dripping wet, some still trailing umbilical cords, and were placed in a pen close to the fire. The adult goats outside, from whom they had been separated, set up a chorus of protest. The Senussi took great care to protect these little creatures from the severe cold of winter evenings in North Africa. Livestock was their only real source of wealth. I had once seen a deserted but perfectly good house, of the type built pre-war by Italian colonists, which was occupied by sheep and goats while their master lived as usual in his tent pitched outside.

* * *

Next morning, as I was preparing to leave, an elderly Arab entered the tent in the company of a teenage girl, probably his granddaughter. He motioned me to sit down beside them and then proceeded to warn me of all the dangers around us; he seemed genuinely concerned for my welfare. He then started praying and, pointing a finger above his head, assured me of the protection of Allah. I responded by showing him a small wooden crucifix which always hung around my neck. He recognized this symbol of Christianity and kissed it several times. Senussis were deeply religious people, part of a strong fraternity of Muslims. They frequently mentioned the name of their leader, Idris, who was then in exile. His absence seemed a matter of great concern to them.

I appreciated the old man's kindness but confess I felt happier when he turned his attention from my spiritual to my material needs by despatching the girl with instructions, it seemed, to prepare food; he rightly judged I could do with something to eat before setting out. Soon she was back with a dixie of hot, steaming scrambled egg, which she handed to me together with a spoon – the latter was a rarity. I set about enjoying my first real breakfast. The young girl watched me attentively from start to finish.

She then asked me to take off my boots and give them to her. At first I was a bit reluctant to comply with this request, not knowing if it had some significance. But the old man, sensing my doubts, assured me it was quite in order, so I handed them over. In fact, she simply proceeded to give them a good coating of fat. They had carried me 150 miles or more over rough country in rain and sun and were in dire need of maintenance.

Grateful as I was for all this attention, time was pressing and I was anxious to get away. I confess I was also just a shade preoccupied about the attentions of the young girl. I was not acquainted with Arab customs and felt I had indulged their hospitality quite enough. The last thing I wanted to do was to give offence in any way; I had problems enough!

I need not have worried. When the old man saw I was determined to go, he searched among his belongings and produced a tin of meat – Italian Army issue – which he insisted on my accepting as a parting gift. I tried my best to express my thanks to these poor but generous people. Once again the old man gave me his blessing, and then, a little sadly, I took my leave of them both.

* * *

By the end of that day I had reached a position somewhere south of Derna. I had known Derna; it was a pretty coastal resort reached by descending a long winding road from the escarpment above it. We had once spent a couple of days there comfortably billeted in a disused hotel. But there would be no British troops there now. It was not a place worth defending, unlike Tobruk, further east, which had a good harbour and installations.

I had been keeping within sight of the main east-west road on my left throughout the day. On one occasion I had been able to move in close enough to observe and note the formation markings on passing vehicles. I had made no contact with local people and when darkness came I decided not to seek food but to continue on my way and put another ten miles behind me during the night.

* * *

In the morning I found that the road which had been on my left all along, was veering right and running across my front. In order, therefore, to keep to my line of march, I would have to cross it.

This road was in open country and, being the only metalled one, was in constant use by vehicles travelling to and from the front. Crossing it would present no problem at night, but now, in broad daylight, I would have to find somewhere with sufficient bushes or trees on both sides of the road to provide concealment for an approach. With this in mind I pressed on, keeping the road in sight from a safe distance.

In due course I came to a narrow elevated ridge covered with trees and bushes which ran right across the road at right angles. At the point of intersection there was a cutting in the ridge to facilitate the passage of the road over it. This suggested itself as an ideal place to cross.

I therefore mounted the ridge and crept cautiously along it between lulls in the passing traffic until I reached the top of the cutting, where I lay down and waited. From this vantage point I could watch vehicles coming and going in both directions. It was not long before a moment came when traffic had disappeared altogether on both sides. The highway was at once empty and silent. Now was my chance.

I jumped up, scrambled through some shrub, slid down the short embankment and landed heavily on the road. But in that split second I was stopped abruptly in my tracks, stunned and shocked. There right before my eyes, just a few yards away, was a solitary German soldier sitting motionless astride a stone bolder, a rifle across his knees. From where I had lain, above the cutting, he had been hidden from my view. By the lost look on his face he must have been taken as much by surprise as I had been.

In this situation I could only feign unconcern. I continued on my way across the road and mounted the opposite bank. I did not get far. The German sprang to life, and I heard a click from the bolt of his rifle followed by a somewhat plaintive call, 'Halt!' I turned round. He was now standing on the road, feet apart, with his rifle aimed at me from the hip. Slowly I descended and came towards him. He again shouted, 'Halt!' We stood there staring at each other across the road. He was young, probably still in his teens; his pale face bore an anxious expression. 'Englander?', he asked in a shaky voice. I nodded.

There was the sound of an approaching vehicle. A covered truck appeared, slowed down and stopped in front of us. German soldiers jumped down from the tailboard and came over. My young captor seemed relieved. Still keeping me covered, he explained the situation to the new arrivals. They were clearly nonplussed, gazing at me almost in disbelief. Then as voices were raised in an excited exchange of words, an NCO stepped forward and politely ordered me into the back of the truck. The others followed. My 150-mile trek across enemy territory lasting twelve days had suddenly ended. Two more days might well have seen me clear, but that was no comfort now.

The vehicle started up and drove off westwards in the direction of Barce, ever further away from the front. I was a 'prisoner of war'.

Chapter 8

In Enemy Hands

As I was carried off in that truck, I think I suffered a sort of mental paralysis. I was numbed by the realization of what had just happened. I reflected on the two years' hard training and preparation that had been invested in me to do an important job and which, at a stroke, had been written off. I felt guilty and ashamed at the terrible and utter waste of it all. I was suddenly a useless, almost helpless being, a parasite destined to be fed and housed until some day, mercifully, I should be set free.

My mood was not shared by my high-spirited captors, who were eager to engage me in conversation. They were burning with curiosity about so many things and plied me with a barrage of questions. Why were Indian troops fighting with us? How did you became a captain after only two years' service? What are the exact words of the song 'Siegfried Line'? What are the girls like in Cairo? Why don't you get fresh bread in the front line like German soldiers? The latter question was posed by a bumptious individual who, nevertheless, was filling his mouth with British army biscuits and corned beef, obviously captured rations, while speaking disdainfully about them. In response, I produced my tin of Italian meat given me by the old Arab and proceeded to eat its contents with equally disparaging remarks about it. The others were amused, even if he was not.

* * *

There was only one interruption to an otherwise smooth journey back to Barce. We were about half way there and the truck was speeding along the metalled road in open country. Suddenly the driver applied his brakes fiercely and yelled, 'Raf!' The vehicle screeched to a halt as the occupants tumbled out and scurried across the road. I remained put. Almost immediately there was a roar of engines overhead and, peering over the tailboard, I recognized one of our Blenheim bombers. It thundered past flying perilously low following the line of the road, presumably on its way home from a mission. At that moment its rear gunner must have spotted us for he gave us a burst from his machine gun. Bullets spattered the road, ricocheted off the steel sides of the truck and tore through the canvas canopy above my head as I lay on the floor of the vehicle. It was all over in a matter of seconds and no one was hurt. The Germans came rushing back, laughing and excited, no doubt relieved at their escape.

With everyone back on board we resumed the journey. But the atmosphere in the company had changed. Their pride had been dented by my witnessing them scuttling away unceremoniously before the threat of British guns. For my part, I was able to hold my head just a little higher.

Before reaching Barce, where I expected to be searched and interrogated, I gave away my binoculars and compass, much to the delight of the recipients in the truck. At least this might ensure that they did not get into official hands to be used against us. I was sorry to part with the field glasses; they bore an inscription, 'Please return to ... after the war'. I do not recall the name and address of this public-spirited person who had tried to help the war effort, but I would like to think he got them back eventually.

* * *

'Name, rank and number is all you are obliged to give if you are taken prisoner', reads an army training manual. Later that morning, when I was confronted by an interrogating officer, an infantry major, I stuck to the book. He noted the brief details I had given him but then proceeded to make a rather clumsy attempt to sound me out on names of units. I presume he was unaccustomed to this sort of duty, as my stony silence embarrassed him and he quickly changed the subject. He then broached the matter of German casualties and was anxious to know if I could provide him with the names of any of their men who had been taken prisoner recently. I knew, in fact, the name of just one, a Catholic army chaplain called Frense. He had been taken prisoner with a small group of

German soldiers near Bardia during our November advance. My platoon had the task of guarding them temporarily until they could be escorted down the line. Padre Frense had pleaded with me for hot food for his comrades, but I had to explain that none had been delivered to my own soldiers for several days and we could offer only tinned beef and biscuits. When he found that I was a Roman Catholic, we had some common ground and we talked for quite a while. In the course of our conversation I had learned his name.

When I mentioned the padre's name to my interrogator he was on the telephone immediately, and before long two senior army chaplains burst into the room, gave the 'Heil Hitler' greeting and pressed me for more information about Kriegspfarrer Frense. Apparently he had been officially reported killed in action, so naturally they were overjoyed by the good tidings I had brought.

Many years later, I came across his name again, in a book written by a German commander in the desert. He described Kriegspfarrer Frense being taken prisoner and went on to say that he was the scourge of his keepers whilst in captivity. Mention was made of a gallant but abortive attempt by Axis prisoners to hijack the troopship in which they were sailing from Suez to South Africa. The good padre, it seems, was the brains behind it all.

* * *

Barce, at that time, must have been some kind of administrative headquarters, unused to the sudden appearance of enemy prisoners of war. My arrival caused a mild stir, judging by the number of German officers who came to see me, probably out of curiosity. They were keen to draw me into discussion on the war and the prospects for peace. At that particular moment their fortunes had reached a high watermark; their armies were advancing well into Russia, while their new allies, the Japanese, had achieved resounding successes in the Far East, not the least of which was the recent sinking of two of our capital warships; and here in Africa the Germans were once more riding the crest of a wave. So altogether they had good reason to be confident about a quick and successful conclusion to the war. For my part, I could not help feeling depressed by their high spirits and cockiness.

Among the various visitors was a senior medical officer who spoke perfect English. He produced a British army pamphlet on tropical diseases and told me he was translating it for distribution to the Afrika Corps as they had nothing like it. He then proceeded to harangue me about the futility of this war, making the sort of comments I was to hear repeated many times by others: 'If only you would get rid of the warmonger Churchill we could all have peace. Why does Britain continue with this useless war? Surely you must realize that you cannot win it. We Germans and yourselves are racially the same and we should be allies, not enemies. Just think what we could achieve with a combination of the German army and the British navy! We could conquer the world!'

They had a blind faith in victory which matched ours; and just as we could not believe that any free-thinking German really supported Hitler, so they were firmly convinced that Churchill was a tyrant leading a lot of misguided and unwilling followers to their doom.

* * *

During my three days in Barce I was kept under permanent guard in a German sergeants' mess. I dined at their table and slept in the same room. They were friendly and courteous. Every evening after supper an accordion was produced and the company would break into boisterous drinking songs. I suspect that a little extra fervour was added for my benefit. Certainly their morale was high at that time compared with ours, while their faith in Rommel and confidence in ultimate victory were unquestionable.

My only possessions of any value were a wristwatch and a gold signet ring. My hosts warned me that I would probably be relieved of them as I passed through the thieving hands of those in the rear areas. I was amused to hear them speak in derogatory terms about their colleagues in the safe spots clear of the combat zone, just as our own men did. The 'base wallahs' were always suspected of getting double cigarette rations and enjoying the pick of welfare supplies and comforts. It may not have been true, but the front line troops on both sides seemed to take it for granted.

I decided to take some precautions anyway. I recalled the advice given two years earlier at an officers' training unit in Dunbar by a First World War veteran, an ex-PoW with much experience of escapes. He provided many useful tips, one of which I now put to use.

With a borrowed needle and thread I sewed my ring and watch, having first removed the strap, into the lining of the fly button holes of my trousers. This caused much amusement in the mess but equally much admiration when the job was finished. Its first test would come in the prisoner reception unit in Benghazi.

I suppose that after three days the novelty of having a British officer in the mess was wearing a bit thin for these sergeants, especially as they were required to mount guard over me night and day. With only half a dozen or so mess members, this duty was quite a drag. However, when the time came to leave, they all gathered together to see me off. On principle, I did not shake hands with any of them; they were still our enemies, and to remain aloof and stand on one's dignity in this way was one of the few means left to a prisoner to demonstrate that, at least spiritually, he had not come to terms with capitulation. For all that, they had been very decent to me and I made a point of thanking them.

* * *

It was an hour's ride from Barce to Benghazi, where I was to be officially handed over to the Italians. This was routine for all prisoners captured in North Africa, as Axis forces in that theatre of war were under the supreme command of the Italians. My final destination, therefore, would be Italy.

On arrival at Benghazi I was consigned to a huge dockside warehouse, a hangar-like building able to house several hundred inmates. I was its sole occupant. A fortnight before, it must have been overflowing with men trapped and seized in this corner of Libya during Rommel's lightning offensive.

The reality of prisoner status was now firmly brought home to me – interrogations, searches, limited food, locked doors and isolation. The camaraderie and licence of the early days of capture had gone for good.

My solitary confinement in Benghazi did not last long, however; within a week, and in company with some British soldiers recently captured, I was put aboard an open truck and we set off for Tripoli.

It was a very uncomfortable, dusty journey lasting four days, with the monotony occasionally relieved by stops for food and ablutions. In the evenings we halted at barracks or forts, where we were given a hot meal before being locked up for the night.

At one of these staging posts I got into conversation with the Italian major in charge. In flawless English he spoke with nostalgia about his native land, describing the beauty of the countryside around his home in Tuscany, especially now with the approach of spring. No doubt he envied me the prospect of spending the rest of the war peacefully in his beloved homeland. He asked me to join him at supper that night, an invitation I was sorry to decline as I realized he was being genuinely kind. I think my refusal took him by surprise. I gave no reason and hoped he understood.

This officer was typical of the Italians I had the opportunity of speaking to in North Africa. One sensed a weariness and resignation. They had, after all, been campaigning on and off in these parts for over a decade, and success had come slowly. The Germans, by comparison, being new to the desert, were fresh and keen and notably flushed with their easy victories in Western and Eastern Europe. They had their hearts in the struggle and were solidly behind their leaders. The Italian soldier, however, was not much motivated by the grand design of Il Duce and had little stomach in fighting for a cause about which his countrymen seemed politically divided anyway.

* * *

We finally fetched up at our destination, a large transit camp outside Tripoli at a place called Tarhuna. This is where prisoners were held pending availability of shipping to take them from the port of Tripoli across the sea to Naples. After the usual formalities of searches and documentation I was shepherded over to the officers' compound.

Inside were men of many nationalities, regiments and ranks, but before long I was approached and greeted by brother officers of the Welch. Most of them had been taken at Sceleidima or Benghazi three weeks earlier and were anxious to have news of the battle fronts. I had little to give. They told me that Corporal Shaw and Private Jones had pitched up there the week before and that until they did, there had been wild rumours about the fate of the three of us. It was comforting to be back among friends, but I was saddened by the wretched, humiliating state to which they had been reduced.

With the numbers involved, Tarhuna Camp suffered from shortage of space. But never was this more so than at night, when prisoners were jammed tight in limited accommodation with doors and windows sealed. Adding to the discomfort of overcrowding was the nightly unrelenting chorus of snoring. It was everywhere, filling the already heavily polluted and stuffy atmosphere!

Nights were cold, and officers lucky enough to have possession of greatcoats slept in them. Not having one myself, I decided to make up a substitute from a couple of blankets. So, applying myself once more with a borrowed needle and thread, I tailored a garment complete with sleeves, collar and belt. I was well pleased with the result – it was like a short dressing gown – and only hoped the misuse of army blankets might escape the notice of the authorities. I was soon to find out.

Early one morning, whilst it was still dark and cold, we were roused, ushered outside and marched towards a line of parked lorries. Realizing we were on the move again, several officers had wrapped camp blankets around their shoulders, hoping to retain them for the journey. But they were promptly relieved of them as they passed through the checkpoints. I was wearing my new creation and wondering what might happen to it, or possibly me, as a result of my enterprise. To my great delight the sentries motioned me through without a murmur. I had won a coat.

We clambered aboard the waiting trucks and were transported in convoy down to Tripoli docks, where we drew up alongside an Italian freighter. After boarding it we assembled on the open deck for muster parade. A chilly dawn was breaking and I was glad of my makeshift coat.

* * *

The ship was alive with preparations for sailing. Finally, tugs arrived and we cast off. We slipped quietly out of the harbour, picking our way between submerged wrecks. As we emerged into the open sea we were joined by an escort of two destroyers, one on each side.

We learned from the crew that this ship was the last of a line of seven. The others had all been sunk running the gauntlet over this stretch of water between North Africa and Italy. Our vessel seemed well protected, for as well as her armed escorts, the ship itself was bristling with anti-aircraft guns.

Once clear of land, all prisoners were ordered below into the empty cargo holds. It was almost dark inside as the tops of the holds were covered over and battened down. Access to the deck above was by fixed ladders, each leading up through a hole in the hatch cover. There were five or six hundred of us crammed into those holds, and it was obvious that precious few would be able to escape from them in time if the ship should go down quickly. Self-preservation prompted me to settle down on the nearest available space beside the foot of one of the ladders.

We had been under way for only half an hour when the ship's engines started to slow down. The noise and vibration thankfully abated and finally stopped altogether. To our surprise, we were then allowed up on deck again, only to find that we were back once more in Tripoli.

Food rations for the day were issued – one large and very hard ship's biscuit per head. We spent the rest of the day watching the activities of the port until it was dusk, when we were sent below again while the ship moved off for the second time. We assumed that the presence of the British navy had thwarted the first attempt to leave port.

* * *

The sea was not rough but the ship rolled enough to affect those easily given to sickness, which made the already foul smell of a ship's hold even worse. Unpleasant as it was to be confined, like rats in a hole, it was the danger outside which preoccupied our minds. An occasional loud clanging on the deck above was unnerving, just as sudden unusual noises can be when flying in an aircraft.

* * *

That first night seemed very long, and it was a great relief when morning came and we were permitted to climb up on to the open decks once more. After the darkness of the holds, the brightness of the sun on the sea was at first blinding. But the fresh air after the stench below was heavenly.

By midday we were completely out of sight of land and sailing along peacefully in the company of our two destroyers close by on each side. Suddenly there was a great commotion. Loud blasts from the ship's siren sent the crew scurrying to action stations. The anti-aircraft gunners, perched above us, hastily strapped on their helmets and swung the gun turrets round to the port side. Shrill whistle signals prompted the guards to run around shouting orders at us, trying to herd us below decks as quickly as possible. I strained my eyes trying to discover what was happening. I was in no hurry to get below.

Away on the horizon, flying silently almost at sea level, a squadron of aircraft was approaching. A shot rang out from one of the destroyers. Immediately a single aircraft disengaged from the formation, climbed up into the sky and released recognition signal flares. It had been a false alarm; they were Axis planes. They continued to fly low over the water and disappeared behind us.

There had been a few moments of silent apprehension broken by a rising hubbub of voices from the crowded decks as soon as the danger had gone. I thought of occasions in the past when we had rejoiced at the radio news of enemy shipping being sunk attempting to run the blockade on which we now found ourselves. I suspect we viewed things a little differently just then.

* * *

Throughout the next day considerable numbers of depth charges were dropped, creating shock waves which thumped against the hull of our ship and sent rattling vibrations along the metal railings and ladders. British submarines may have been in the vicinity, but no attack was made on our small convoy and our journey continued uninterrupted.

Before nightfall we sighted land, our first glimpse of the Italian coastline. Word went round that we were heading for Palermo in Sicily. Later that night, when we were back in the holds, the ship ceased rolling and her engines were shut down. When morning came and we emerged once more on deck we found that we had already reached the shelter of the harbour at Palermo and had dropped anchor.

There were rumours from the crew that submarines had been trailing us for two days and that this diversion into port was an attempt to shake them off. Anyway, we remained there all day waiting for darkness to fall before heading out to sea again.

In the early hours of our fifth day aboard I succeeded in climbing up on deck with a few others just for a breath of fresh air, and what a wonderful spectacle awaited us! We were steaming towards the Bay of Naples, and in the distant darkness, way ahead of us, we could see Vesuvius, clearly outlined by a mantle of burning lava. The volcano was in eruption – a rare sight. A guard kindly let us stay, so we stood there watching, fascinated. When dawn came, the brightness of the sun gradually outshone the fires, revealing a pall of black smoke rising above the summit.

As we drew nearer to Naples, the destroyers, having completed their task, signalled with their sirens that they were taking leave of us. Our ship sounded her siren in acknowledgement as the escorts swung away and headed back to sea and the war. Reducing speed, we continued to creep forward ever deeper into the bay. It was a beautiful morning, clear and calm, as we edged slowly into the port and finally tied up alongside.

It seemed a new world. The desert and its war were now only memories.

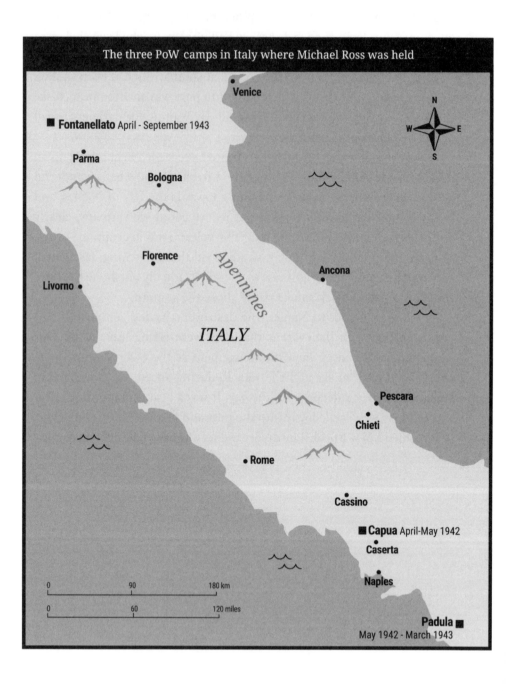

The three PoW camps in Italy where Michael Ross was held

■ **Fontanellato** April - September 1943

Parma

Bologna

Venice

N
W   E
S

Florence

Apennines

Ancona

Livorno

ITALY

Pescara

Chieti

Rome

Cassino

■ **Capua** April-May 1942

Caserta

Naples

0   90   180 km
0   60   120 miles

Padula ■
May 1942 - March 1943

Part II

A Prisoner

12ª Feb 42.
(post mark date)
(Data del timbro postale)

My dear, *Mother + Margaret.*

I am well (I have not been wounded (or) ~~I have been~~
Sto   bene   (non   sono   stato   ferito   (o)   sono   stato

~~slightly wounded)~~. I am a prisoner of the Italians and I am
ferito   leggermente).   Sono stato   catturato   dagli   Italiani   e   mi

being treated well.
trovo   bene.

Shortly I shall be transferred to a prisoner's camp and
Nei   prossimi   giorni   sarò   trasferito   in   un   campo   di

I will let you have my new address.
prigionieri   del   quale   vi   comunicherò   l'indirizzo.

Only then will I be able to receive letters from you
Soltanto   allora   potrò   ricevere   la   vostra   corrispondenza

and to reply.
e   rispondervi.

Michael Ross

With love   (signature)
Saluti affettuosi   (firma)

Michael's family is informed that he has been captured. (*Ross Family Archive*)

Chapter 9

Doom and Gloom

We were back from the wars, but a hero's welcome was not for the likes of us; we were met only by the contemptuous stares of bystanders on the quayside as we were led in groups directly from the ship to a nearby delousing centre. We mustered what dignity we could by showing an arrogant disregard for the onlookers, but the faces of many of us betrayed signs of embarrassment. One could not help feeling discredited and degraded by our present plight; we were, after all, the living proof of our failure, the by-product of an enormous military disaster.

Whatever excuses might be sought for the recent sudden reversal of fortune, there was no denying the tremendous advantage in time and distance enjoyed by the enemy in sustaining the war in North Africa. It had needed a three-month sea voyage for us to reach the battle front out in Libya, while here we were already in the homeland of the enemy after only a few days' journey from the very same front.

Naturally, we were preoccupied with our grave situation, and our morale was low. Yet I confess that any humiliation I may have felt was tempered by a boyish elation at arriving in a strange land with the prospect of new challenges and adventures.

Inside the delousing centre we stripped off and took our first hot shower in months; meanwhile, our clothes were collected and put through a lice-destroying steam pressure boiler. Our hosts were taking no chances; they were well acquainted with the bug-ridden Libyan barracks and old fortresses along the North African coast, occupied and re-occupied in turn by friend and foe alike. By contrast, the surrounding desert was an extraordinarily clean place, devoid of dirt and grime; one's skin remained unsullied for days. The air, too, apart from periodic gunfire, was invariably fresh and unpolluted.

* * *

By the time we had finished showering, our clothes were ready for collection in the changing room. Some of us were due for a surprise, much to the amusement of the others.

No warning had been given, but it was soon evident that anything made of leather put through this cleansing process had permanently shrunk to a fraction of its former size. There was great hilarity as one item after another was discovered: belts now resembling dog collars, gloves barely doll-size, shrivelled up pairs of braces, and wallets no larger than a book of postage stamps. Laughter now came easily, with the release of the tension built up during five anxious days at sea.

The most amusing case was that of an elderly and rather pompous captain. He had the distinction of having been taken prisoner one night while enjoying a game of bridge in his tent with three others at some remote supply outpost. He had wisely taken the opportunity to pack a suitcase containing all the essential comforts for the prisoner of war. Apart from such luxuries as a change of underclothing and soft slippers for evening wear, his pride and joy (and the envy of us all) was a fine pair of riding breeches.

When these reappeared that morning after cleansing, he was dismayed to discover that the leather patches on the inside of each leg had contracted to the size of a large coin. The cloth had consequently been pinched together so tightly that he was unable to pull the breeches on. A helpful guard, seeing his dilemma, came to the rescue. Armed with a sharp jack-knife, he promptly sliced off the remains of the offending leather, with the result that two gaping holes appeared, the size of the original patches. There was unrestrained laughter at the spectacle of the poor man standing crestfallen in his ruined jodhpurs, his knees and thighs rudely exposed.

* * *

With these preliminaries over, we were marched to a dockside railway siding, where we boarded a train. A tin of meat and a roll of brown bread were issued to everyone and consumed in silence while awaiting departure. It was an hour before the sharp jolting of the carriages heralded the arrival of an engine. The train then pulled out of the docks, passed through the back streets of Naples and finally emerged into the Italian countryside.

Armed guards occupied the train corridors, one to each compartment. They had orders to keep all windows securely closed, as jumping from trains was a popular method of escape. It was a hot day, and soon we were sweating uncomfortably in the stuffy atmosphere. However, we were quick to discover that most of these guards could be bribed or intimidated into modifying their orders, and it was not long before fresh air was coming in freely through open windows.

These men, seemingly of a lower military category than their comrades at the front, were not motivated by the prospect of a glorious conclusion to the war. They showed little interest in its progress and were not over-concerned about its outcome. Despite the constant pressure of Fascist propaganda in the press and on the radio, their only wish was to get back to their homes and families. The tedium of the daily round of guard duties must have added to their indifference. The mainstay of their discipline was the threat of punishment or of transfer to the Russian front.

* * *

Our destination was Capua, an inland town a few hours' train ride from Naples, where a sprawling hutted camp, built to hold a thousand or more prisoners, awaited us. New arrivals from North Africa were held here pending transfer to permanent camps elsewhere. In our case, the chances were that we were in for a long stay, as it was obvious that new camps could not be found overnight for the sudden influx of large numbers of prisoners after our recent defeats in the desert.

'The golden rule for the prisoner is to do only one thing at a time', were the first words of advice given me by a young New Zealand lieutenant. He was propped up in bed, reading, when I entered the hut and he had greeted me with, 'Hiya sport, bad luck', – the sort of remark a batsman might expect on returning to the pavilion after being given out. He had already been a prisoner for six months which gave him a certain status over new arrivals like myself. Having been 'in the bag' long enough to receive a parcel from home, he possessed the trappings of the old hand: a framed photograph of his girlfriend, new shaving kit, fountain pen, knitted cardigan and woollen socks. But more important, he had a coveted and closely guarded small hoard of tinned milk, tea and sugar, the residue of a Red Cross food parcel.

There were several of his kind who for various reasons were having to endure a prolonged stay at this transit camp. On the whole they were an unsociable lot, keeping much to themselves. New friendships meant associating with 'have-nots', which could only be a liability. Little sympathy was shown to the underprivileged newcomer unless you happened to belong to their old outfit or regiment, in which case you might be honoured by an invitation to tea. It was evident that charity was already proving the least enduring of the cardinal virtues.

Few PoWs have recorded their experiences without praising the work of the Red Cross Society in supplying food parcels to the camps. The benefits of those parcels to the prisoner in terms of his physical wellbeing and morale were inestimable. The arrival in camp of a consignment of these eagerly awaited parcels was cause of great rejoicing, positively the highlight of our existence. If such occasions could have been witnessed by those good people whose voluntary efforts and generous donations made it all possible, I think they would have felt duly rewarded.

Red Cross parcels originated at home and were despatched in bulk to Switzerland, from where they were distributed to the camps. They were of a standard size and content and were intended to supplement the local prison diet with such items as tinned meat or fish, cheese, milk, sugar, tea, chocolate and dried fruit, as well as soap and cigarettes which were particularly scarce in wartime Italy. There were some parcels labelled 'Medical', and these were allocated to the sick, as they contained vitaminized food and drink. The aim of the Society was to provide one parcel a week to every prisoner, but problems of transportation through occupied Europe meant supplies were frequently erratic; two issues in our first four months proved, fortunately, exceptional.

These early days of prison life spent in the dreary atmosphere of Capua were for me, and I think many others, the most unhappy and demoralizing of all. The shock of capture and the humiliating experience of being disarmed and incarcerated were still fresh in our minds, whilst inescapable feelings of guilt continued to plague us. Such sentiments affected the soldier more than the sailor whose ship had been sunk or the airman whose plane had been shot down. There was no grey area of doubt for them; they did not have to defend their status as prisoners of war. The soldier, by contrast, had laid down his arms, and whilst this was almost invariably on the orders of a senior commander finding his men in a hopeless situation and anxious to save life or prevent suffering, it was, for the individual, surrender none the less.

I suppose one could draw limited comfort from the thought that even prisoners imposed demands on the enemy's resources and manpower. Indeed, some prisoners exerted considerable pressure in this respect by their persistent attempts at escaping, and in a few tragic instances paid with their lives for doing so. The unpalatable truth remained that here we were, the most able-bodied section of the community to whom so much had been entrusted, now neutralized and relegated to the sidelines like chess pieces removed from the board. It was difficult to stomach the fact that our comrades at the front and even our families at home continued to be exposed to the hostility of an enemy who was now protecting us.

Our social behaviour underwent dramatic changes during those early days in prison. Personal relationships, previously normal, suddenly showed strain. Individuals became markedly insular, withdrawing from their former large groups and associating strictly in twos or threes. These small parties hung together, keeping entirely to themselves to the exclusion of others. Strangers were shunned and absolutely no attempt was made to form new friendships. This splintering and isolation no doubt reduced the area of possible friction within the community as a whole, but it produced the undesirable side-effect of spreading mistrust and suspicion. I deplored this drift from the once cordial general atmosphere but, all the same, I found myself caught up in the situation and started to feel an intense dislike of certain people and groups. By contrast, the individuals within each group trusted each other implicitly, making a fetish of doing everything together and of sharing absolutely everything.

Possibly deep feelings of insecurity had led to these changes; perhaps unconsciously, men were seeking the intimacy and protection of the family group against the larger unfriendly outside world. I suspect that being deprived of responsibilities, except for oneself, and having lost any immediate purpose in life, coupled with fear for the future and the realization that one was powerless to influence or shape it in any way, led men to turn in upon themselves and give priority to their own comfort and survival.

This anti-social behaviour was not just the product of mental anxieties. It had been generated, too, by physical deprivations, above all by the lack of sufficient food. Hunger became a disruptive force, cracking the delicate veneer of good manners and etiquette and exposing men's weaknesses and greed.

Food became an obsession, occupying our daily thoughts and much of our conversation; it was an endless source of interest and concern. Officers were particularly badly off since, under the Geneva Convention, they were not allowed to work and consequently were restricted to the local civilian non-working ration scale; meagre fare indeed for hard-trained, fit men in the prime of life, as we liked to regard ourselves. It was less than half the working ration scale allotted to other ranks, who, in theory, were available for working parties. It was inevitable that this disparity should give rise to a system of barter between ranks, a practice which was to loom large in our lives.

Officers and other ranks were held in separate compounds at Capua, but when an opportunity presented itself, articles of clothing and other valuables would find their way into the men's compound, while loaves of bread would filter back in return. Market rates of exchange for cigarettes, food, etc. soon established themselves; an airman's flying jacket, for example, could fetch almost anything. It was an item greatly coveted by our guards who, unknown to their officers, would offer considerable quantities of black market food in exchange.

The majority of us in those early days had nothing to barter, and it was heartening to find that quite a number of soldiers in my regiment passed over bread to their own officers without payment. I have no doubt this happened with other units too. It spoke a lot for loyalty at a time when, in all honesty, respect for officers by other ranks was at its lowest ebb.

Capua was about as miserable a place as could be, especially when it rained and the distant Apennines were lost in the gloom; one really felt isolated then, particularly as contact with the world outside had been virtually severed. The realities of lost liberty were beginning to bite. Rumours abounded, and any official news of the war that did seep through was invariably cheerless and only compounded our despondency. Looking to the future offered little comfort.

A regular visitor to our lines was the Italian camp chaplain. He would drift in and out of the huts dressed in his black cassock decorated with colourful military epaulettes and with a wide brimmed hat tilted precariously on the back of his bald head. He had a bulky figure, no chin and wore heavily magnifying spectacles. His damp, limp handshake was something to be avoided.

His mission, I suppose, was to try and raise our spirits. He would come in, sit on the edge of a bed, gather a group around him and endeavour to converse in broken English in his rasping voice. The less charitable among us voiced suspicion of his motives and counselled caution in what was said to him. Nevertheless, we welcomed his visits as he was our only direct contact with the authorities, and we used him mercilessly to vent our feelings and make known our numerous complaints. But he proved singularly resilient and returned time and again quite undaunted.

One morning he came bearing news of the sinking of one of the ships which had left Tripoli three days after ours. It too was laden with PoWs, most of whom were lost. It had been torpedoed off Sicily by a British submarine. This appalling news brought a temporary halt to our remonstrations; we started counting our blessings.

* * *

It was my good fortune to enjoy a respite from the dreariness and discontent of Capua. One day, unexpectedly, the camp doctor decided I was to go into hospital. Since capture, I had been suffering from a severe pain in my side which seemed to worsen especially when I lay down. It was decided to investigate. So with other patients I was duly despatched, under escort, by ambulance to the military hospital at Caserta, 12 miles away.

On arrival, we were taken up to the PoW ward, which consisted of some top floor rooms segregated from the rest of the hospital. Sentries mounted guard in the corridors outside. The windows of our ward looked out on to blank walls, so our isolation was complete.

I was in a room with three others, one of whom was a brother officer of the Welch, Tom Pepper, whom I had not seen for several months. He was recovering from gunshot wounds. Hanging above our beds was a crucifix, to one side of which was a portrait of Mussolini and to the other, a portrait of Hitler. 'Christ between two thieves' was the popular local joke among staff.

My stay in hospital coincided with Easter. Being a Roman Catholic, I was given permission to attend Mass, so on Easter Sunday morning an orderly called for me and we went down together to the hospital chapel. It was already crowded, but we got inside and stood in the aisle. What a marvellous sight it was, flowers everywhere and the altar ablaze with candles. The service was in progress, there was the scent of burning incense and from the choir came the music of Bach's mass.

I was moved to feel a part of what had been for me such a familiar scene in times past. But then, looking around, I became aware of a number of young men in the congregation who had been disfigured and dismembered by our acts of war. I was saddened by the sight, and my sense of identity with those around me was lost; I felt an intruder.

I have no doubt that prayers for victory were being offered up that morning by these good Christians, just as they must have been in our churches at home. The meaning of the words I once heard from an army chaplain were now impressed upon me more clearly: 'Fight to win but pray for peace.'

After Mass we returned directly to the ward. It had been, for me, the most poignant Easter service I had ever attended, but I was glad to have been there. On arriving back, I described to my colleagues my brief encounter with the outside world. It prompted one of them to remark, 'You RCs do quite well, you seem to get all the perks in this country!'

The halcyon days in Caserta were soon, alas, brought to an end for me. One morning the senior surgeon, an elderly, bluff, jovial character with red cheeks and wild grey hair, pressed his ear against my chest and back – he seldom used a stethoscope – and pronounced me fit to return to the rigours of prison. Within the hour I was squatting between two guards in the back of a draughty truck with the remains of a Red Cross parcel under my arm, bound for Capua.

* * *

Back in prison, I was greeted with the news that we were shortly to move to a permanent camp in an ancient monastery known as Certosa di San Lorenzo, located in southern Italy at a place called Padula. Our Italian liaison officer described it to us as one of the country's national monuments, set among the lower reaches of the Apennines in the beautiful valley of Diano. He promised that we would find the accommodation, recreational facilities and catering quite superb, and impressed upon us how fortunate we were to be going to such a place.

Predictions like this had to be judged against a tendency for Italians to overrate good things and underrate the bad. I had observed how they delighted in bringing good tidings and raising hopes about something just to make you feel better about it. If things did not work out as expected, the reaction would be, 'Ah, that's fate.' Equally, they were ready to accept, uncritically, forecasts of doom. Thus buffeted between extremes, it was not easy for them to steer an even course through life's ups and downs.

They readily supported a cause or argument on the thinnest evidence and were quick to accept assurances of good things to come, which led to frequent disappointments when the truth emerged. They hoped for miracles and hankered after a promised land which always seemed to elude them. They contrasted the good fortune of others with their own wretchedness, and were firm believers in the grass being greener on the other side of the fence. But although they had little confidence in the future of their country, they still retained the strongest sentimental attachment to it.

The Italians had reason to feel disillusioned and to be demoralized. Instead of the quick victory promised by Mussolini, the end of the war was nowhere in sight; their African possessions were lost and they were now sharing the disasters of a Russian adventure with the Germans, for whom they had little love or trust.

But there were other Italians, a minority who regarded the sufferings and humiliations of the present war as the necessary price to pay for the overthrow of a hated regime; and these people, by contrast, had unquestioning faith and hope in the future.

Chapter 10

Inmates of a Monastery in Southern Italy

The day of departure arrived, and it was with light hearts and great expectations that we finally shook the dust of Capua from our feet and boarded a train for Padula.

Our route took us south again through Naples, where we were shunted temporarily into a siding to clear the line for an approaching troop train. It rushed passed us heading towards the port, crammed full of noisy German soldiers. Following behind was a freight train loaded with armoured vehicles in sand-coloured paint. For a moment one sensed again the urgent business of war, but we could no longer feel part of it. We were only spectators, we had no cause to sing like the lusty soldiers we had just seen. Yet they were en route to the front while we were retreating to the peace of the countryside.

It was a glorious sunny morning as we resumed our journey. The route included a broad sweep around the base of the volcano Vesuvius, still slowly smouldering, a brief glimpse of part of the ruins of Pompeii and, later on, after emerging from a tunnel high up in the mountains, a bird's eye view of distant Salerno with its whitewashed buildings along the coast and the vast expanse of shimmering blue sea beyond. It could all have been a tourist's dream tour.

By early afternoon we reached Padula. We detrained at a tiny railway station and looked around with curiosity. The country air smelled good. Soon we were marching off along a dusty lane in a long column, our backs a little straighter than for some time. Peasants dotted about the fields, mainly women in wide straw hats, paused in their tasks to gaze at us with expressionless faces.

There was no mistaking the monastery. It stood solidly in isolation on a gentle slope at the foot of a range of mountains. Immediately behind and towering above it was the village of Padula, its stone buildings clinging limpet-like to the crest of a hill.

As we drew near, the resident Italian soldiery, our guardians-to-be, gathered around the gates, curious to inspect their new charges. We passed through a forecourt and approached the main entrance to the building. It was fortress-like and above it, carved in stone, was an inscription intended for the fraternity of years gone by – it reminded them that they were forsaking the world. Such sentiments were hardly lost on us. After clattering along cobbled stone passages we emerged into the sun-drenched central courtyard of the monastery. This was journey's end and we flopped down, glad to rest.

The courtyard was rectangular, some 100yds by 50yds in size. It was enclosed on all four sides by a two-storey building. Incorporated in this building, behind a series of pillars and arches, was an unbroken cloister running right around the courtyard – it was said to be the longest in Europe. The floor above it consisted of long, narrow dormitories each the length of its side of the courtyard – we called them wings. Junior officers were to occupy these. There were also smaller but more numerous rooms at ground level. They opened out on to the cloisters and were assigned to senior officers.

The windows of the four wings faced inwards overlooking the courtyard; the back walls had no windows. This denial of visual contact with the outside world no doubt accorded with the discipline of the former occupants; now, less willingly, it was ours.

The courtyard itself was grassed over. It had a large bowl-like, obsolete fountain at its centre, from which radiated gravel paths reaching to the cloisters.

But we had little reason to complain; we were not constrained. The monastery had space, including an additional recreation area which we called the paddock. This was a field about the size of a small football pitch fringed with olive trees and situated immediately outside the wall of the south wing on the opposite side of the monastery from the village and mountains. Access to the paddock was directly from the courtyard through an archway flanked by two beautiful, curving, stone and marble stairways which led up to the dormitories.

* * *

The field became the scene of some tough, boisterous ball games, but it also served as a quiet, peaceful retreat, especially on hot summer afternoons, when most men were indoors taking the customary siesta. In that hour it was good to lie undisturbed beneath the shade of the olive trees and enjoy the sound of insects, the smell of the grass and the sight of the monastery and mountains. One could forget the barbed wire and ignore the listless sentries surveying the scene from their watchtowers.

Many prisoners found Padula a depressing place; certainly it was bleak and cheerless during the constant rains and cold of that first spring. Despite the discomfort, for me the monastery evoked a feeling of serenity. Its architecture was imposing and the surrounding unspoilt countryside and mountainous landscape quite beautiful.

* * *

Having settled in and taken stock of our new home, we quickly set about organizing our lives within the limits permitted us. The Geneva Convention laid down rules which the Italian authorities complied with scrupulously. Apart from being over-cautious about security, which we often found irksome, they did their best to make life as tolerable as possible.

Orders from the Italian commandant were passed on to us through the Senior British Officer (SBO). As in any normal army unit, camp orders, containing instructions and general information, were posted up daily under the authority of the SBO. He appointed a small staff from among the prisoners to assist in the day-to-day running of the domestic affairs of the camp.

Within the area of the monastery allotted for our own use, and to which we were strictly confined, we were virtually independent. We were responsible for our own kitchens, catering arrangements, camp cleaning, etc. To assist in this, a contingent of British other ranks, volunteers from PoW camps elsewhere in Italy, were assigned to us. Our own doctors, dentists and chaplains looked after our physical and spiritual needs, using equipment and facilities provided by the Italians.

The only demand made on us by the authorities was to parade for roll call whenever they thought fit, normally twice a day, and to be in bed by 'lights out'. Later on during the night, the Italian duty officer would walk around, visiting each room to take a head count.

The Italians were, of course, responsible for overall organization and maintenance and for the supply and storage of food and materials. The workshops, offices, laundries and quarters of the permanent staff and guards were situated in the administrative buildings of the monastery immediately behind the north wing facing the village. This entire area was out of bounds to us.

We ran a small shop where such things as writing materials, local newspapers and toilet requisites could be obtained in exchange for a special camp scrip, equivalent to Italian lire. We received our army pay in this currency each month after deductions for the cost of our food. Records of pay were sent to the UK every month, and balances, if any, were credited to our bank accounts. Unfortunately, the high charge for the basic food ration plus the cost of occasional items bought for us on the local black market, together with an unfavourable rate of exchange, meant there was often little to show at the end of the month. It was a matter of concern, especially for married men with dependants.

Gambling debts, sometimes well beyond an officer's Army pay, resulting in the main from card-playing marathons, were settled by personal letters to banks at home requesting transfer of funds. At one point, indebtedness started to get so out of hand that the SBO wisely intervened and put a stop to this practice altogether.

* * *

The first two months of captivity spent in transit camps had been a period of stagnation and inaction. Now, however, with a recreation field and covered cloisters where one could exercise freely, regardless of the weather, there was a sudden urge to get fit again. Men threw themselves into a variety of physical activities. But it proved a flash in the pan. 'It just makes me hungry for food that isn't there,' was a typical comment.

Food certainly was the major problem. Whilst Padula had brought improvements in many ways, food was not one of them. The meagre ration scale remained unchanged, and it was several months before we saw a Red Cross parcel. Having normally enjoyed a healthy appetite, I found the constant feelings of hunger hard to bear; for big men it must have been worse. Almost everyone had lost weight. Understandably, this particular malaise did not appear to affect our kitchen staff. In fact, the indications were they were putting on weight! But a further, less commendable, instance of private hogging once came to light. It concerned a small group of mainly senior officers, who were found to have been appropriating extra food in secret for some time from the black market through the agency of an Italian NCO acting on his own. Private trafficking of this sort was forbidden. Whenever black market food was available locally, the policy was to purchase it officially for the benefit of the camp as a whole. So the offending officers were duly reprimanded by the SBO, and their Italian accomplice was promptly demoted and sacked by the Italian Commandant.

There was one famous occasion when a major on the commandant's staff managed to procure for us, on the Milan black market, half a dozen barrels of sweetened condensed milk. Now this was the most highly prized of all foods in a PoW camp – normally it was available only in small quantities from Red Cross parcels – so it represented a marvellous bonus. Undoubtedly, our Italian commandant took considerable risks in authorizing the purchase for us.

Unfortunately, on arrival, one barrel slipped through the hands of the Italian soldiers hauling it up the steps of the monastery, causing it to crash and burst open. An amusing scene apparently followed, as soldiers rushed around with mess tins endeavouring to scoop up and salvage something from the cascade of precious liquid.

When the consignment was made over to us it was unanimously agreed that it should be rationed out to each individual rather than be allowed to pass through the kitchens. Accordingly, it was deposited in the camp shop, from where it was dispensed, two cupfuls per week per officer, until it was all consumed.

At the time, the shop was in the hands of a couple of South African officers, and it did not escape our notice that they were now spending an unusually long time in the shop after closing hours, behind locked doors, working on their accounts – or so they said. There was also more than a suspicion that they were recovering some of their lost weight. So putting two and two together, it was decided that a change of management might be in the camp's best interest.

* * *

When the cult of physical fitness cult declined, there was an upsurge of enthusiasm for intellectual pursuits of all kinds. Playing games and keeping fit was all very well, but our enforced idleness, it was felt, must be put to better use. We must have something positive to show for it. The demand was clear; we needed a comprehensive educational training scheme.

With the wealth of knowledge and experience of over four hundred officers to call upon, a broad field of subjects was available: languages, history, law, medicine, government, agriculture and other more specialized topics. Training programmes were drawn up, instructors mobilized, student lists made out, times and places of classes decided upon and textbooks sent for from home. Several keen students worked out personal schedules fitting in as many courses as possible. The scheme was launched with great resolution and expectation.

Alas, the high pitch of this feverish activity did not endure. It took just a few short weeks for interest to wane and the size of study groups to diminish noticeably. Excuses came easily: 'I need more free periods' or 'I've decided to concentrate on my Italian.' Within a couple of months the great thirst for knowledge had been slaked and the movement had spent itself. The only reminders of the once tremendous surge of intellectual endeavour were small groups of hard-core enthusiasts dotted here and there about the monastery like pools of water drying out in the sun after a storm. The fact was that in prison camp few people proved to have the will or inclination to undertake sustained study of any kind.

My personal contribution was to tutor a class in shorthand. I had acquired a limited knowledge of the skill during the three-month-long voyage in convoy from the Clyde to Suez the previous year. Prior to embarkation, I had purchased a copy of Pitmans *Teach Yourself Shorthand* with the object of occupying my spare moments at sea. I had certainly not anticipated putting it to use in this way, however.

I was heartened by the ready response of so many pupils anxious to join my class. It was clearly a popular subject, regarded as useful in so many fields; and besides, no previous knowledge was necessary. Unfortunately, there was also a common belief that it could be acquired quickly and easily – experience was soon to dispel that idea. In due course my class suffered the same fate as most of the others. It eroded from an initial twenty to a faithful three in just under a month; even these, I suspect, only persevered out of politeness to me. Finally, with only one pupil left, I called it a day.

The long-suffering last student was a gunner officer called Roy Lowndes, who became a good friend. He was a likeable character, short and chubby with a round cheery face and neat dark wavy hair. He was rarely without a pipe gripped between small perfect teeth. Roy was the most patient and even-tempered of men, able to argue convincingly and express lucidly his strongly held right-wing political views. He had, at one time, been nominated as Conservative candidate for a London constituency, but the war intervened. His hopes of entering Parliament after the war were, in fact, to be fulfilled, and later on he succeeded in making a name for himself in the financial world.

Apart from Roy, I doubt whether any of my students gained much from this experience except, perhaps, to disillusion themselves of the idea that acquiring a skill in shorthand was child's play. On the other hand, it convinced me that there is no better way of learning a subject than by having to teach it.

Later, in midwinter, I attended a course on economics given by an RASC officer, Angus Maude. Conditions on those bleak afternoons were far from ideal. Our classroom was a quiet corner of the draughty cloisters. Angus, quite unperturbed, would hold forth in his croaky voice. He was a frail man with wizened face and a beard, weighed down by an oversize greatcoat, scarf around his neck and trousers hanging over his boots. From time to time he would blow through half-mittened fingers to keep warm. But the class was receptive and held together – a tribute to a teacher who knew his subject and could put it across well. Angus had other talents too: in a camp production of *Twelfth Night* he was a very convincing Malvolio. With his bent figure, spindly stockinged legs and pointed red beard, he was made for the part. Years later, he embarked on a political career and rose to ministerial rank in the government of Mrs Thatcher.

Whilst the formal scheme of educational courses ground to a halt, lectures by experts on individual topics continued to be popular and attracted large audiences, especially if the subject was unusual or thought-provoking. Unlike the set classes, there was no commitment on the part of the person attending; you just brought along a blanket or deckchair, made yourself comfortable and listened. No tiresome questions were asked or homework set, and when you had heard enough you could withdraw with grace.

Oddly enough, talks on military matters had no place in our scheme of things. Despite the wealth and variety of experience to draw upon from men of all three services, including other Commonwealth countries, we just did not want to know. We had no interest in fighting old battles; our concern was for the future only.

It was a different matter, some months later, when the first prisoner from the newly opened Tunis front turned up at Padula. He was immediately required to address the camp on the current war situation, and he had a full house. We had been starved of news from home and were burning for up-to-date information. We were especially concerned about how people in Britain had reacted to our recent disastrous defeat in the desert after such promising victories. Pressed on this, he replied that a typical remark frequently heard was, 'It's strange how the front in North Africa keeps moving forward and backward.' I suspect he was being kind.

* * *

There can be little doubt that the emptiness and futility of life in prison contributed largely to the laziness that became endemic in our society. We had acquired the mentality of the spectator; we looked to be entertained. It was no wonder, then, that activities such as the drama group and choral society attracted a mass following and flourished. There was no waning of enthusiasm here; on the contrary, successive productions went from strength to strength and reached extraordinarily high standards of performance and presentation.

The quality of production was matched by that of the stage sets and props. The inventiveness and ingenuity in improvisation of those behind the scenes more than compensated for the obvious limitations in materials and resources. I was able to help out in the tailoring of costumes, having already acquired some handiness with a needle. But the outstanding exponent, backstage, in the matter of prop production was a Fleet Air Arm pilot known as 'Fingers' Lewis.

Fingers was a slightly built man with a sad face who kept much to himself. He had little hair on the top of his head but could boast the longest beard in the camp. He shuffled about the place in short trousers and a pair of heavy cumbersome flying boots, for which he was sometimes referred to as 'Puss in-Boots'.

There was one famous occasion when Fingers built a miniature stage, about the size of a Punch and Judy theatre, as an advertising gimmick for a forthcoming drama production. It was complete with moving curtains and four changes of scenery. The whole contraption worked automatically, curtains opening, displaying one set for a minute or so, then closing and reopening to show the next one, and so on. The motive power was provided by water flowing from a tap which filled a series of revolving containers connected to a complicated system of pulleys and balances. It was constructed almost entirely from old tins which he had cut, flattened out and remoulded. When put on public view the exhibit proved a star turn in itself and attracted much attention. Its fame travelled far, for even the Italian camp commandant and his staff came over to see it. They smilingly admired Fingers' masterpiece – our guardians were always pleased to find us engaged in innocent pursuits such as this. They did not take so kindly, however, to an equally ingenious creation of Fingers – an air pump – which they were later to discover in an escape tunnel. Fingers' little workshop went out of business.

* * *

There can be no doubt that the opportunity of following some hobby or interest or engaging in some community activity played an important role in maintaining morale and, in the case of more than one individual, preserving their sanity. Such a one was Dick Partridge, a subaltern of my regiment.

Dick was a likeable fellow, stocky, tough, somewhat clumsy and rather scruffy. His flat nose, thick lips and broad hands with nail-bitten fingers gave him the appearance of an out of luck prizefighter. He chain-smoked his monthly ration in a day, dangling a succession of cigarettes precariously from the corner of his mouth. He never removed one to speak but sucked in his breath noisily between sentences. The niceties of etiquette had little interest for Dick, despite his good Welsh county family background. A trifle slow on the uptake, he was the butt of many a joke. But he was resilient, with an abundance of good humour. Dick had no enemies, was the officers' mess favourite and equally popular with his men.

In the months following capture Dick noticeably deteriorated; the familiar grin on his round, plump face disappeared. He just slouched around, coat collar turned up, staring at the ground, ignoring everyone. He lost interest in everything and became a recluse. All attempts to coax him into conversation failed. In PoW language, he was rapidly going 'round the bend'. Even Padre Rees-Davies, the chaplain of our regiment, a small, bright-eyed, cheerful man with the loudest laugh in camp, a person whose constant kindness and high spirits was an example to us all, could do nothing with Dick. But suddenly one morning everything changed; a parcel arrived addressed to Lieut. Partridge.

The sender of that parcel could hardly have guessed at the dramatic change it was to bring to the life of a man at such an advanced stage of depression. Undoubtedly, it saved him. The parcel contained a trumpet, one of Dick's old loves. From the moment he started playing, his morale picked up and his broad smile returned; he was once more sociable and in no time was back to his old self. One could only marvel at his sudden recovery brought about by having this one interest restored to him.

Soon other instruments arrived, and it was not long before a small band was formed. They practised in private and then one evening gave an opening concert. I was operating the stage curtains so was able to peer through from the wings and observe the faces of the audience illuminated in the glow of the footlights. It was fascinating. First, there was an air of quiet expectation, but then when the band struck up, expressions of sheer delight spread across the faces of the entire assembly. The rediscovery of music after such a long absence stirred something in all of us.

Our spiritual needs were well catered for. At one time there were no fewer than eight army chaplains in camp, including a bishop. However, church services, other than Roman Catholic, were poorly attended, despite a total ban on all other camp activities on Sunday mornings. It was only when a chaplain was brave enough to volunteer a lecture or discussion on some aspect of religion that he drew a sizeable audience. Such occasions were too good to be missed by the sceptics, who turned up eager to argue and quick to ridicule. More than one well-meaning padre was obliged to withdraw in embarrassment from these confrontations, never to try again.

The attitude of these noisy minorities was, I think, symptomatic of a wider discontent and loss of faith in authority generally. Prisoners had, I suppose, some reason to feel disillusioned. Many were critical of those in higher authority, believing they had been the victims of their mismanagement or miscalculations. With time on our hands, we not only ruminated at length on the cause and effect of our present plight, but were happy to idle away many an hour examining and questioning some of the fundamental principles on which our society had been built and which we had always taken for granted. Nothing was sacred, but religion in general, and Christianity in particular, were the vulnerable targets which came under constant fire.

I fear that, on the whole, our chaplains, the defenders of the faith, were not equal to this challenge. No doubt it was a daunting task having to contend at close quarters with people who were either stubbornly apathetic or arrogantly anti-religious. Those padres who survived unscathed were either imbued with resolute faith or possessed of an effective intellectual armoury.

There was one padre at Padula undoubtedly blessed with both these qualities. He was a man, much respected, who combined serenity and self-assurance with humility. Before the war he had been a member of an Anglican fraternity somewhere in the West Country, so in his present surroundings he could not have felt too much out of place. In appearance he was parrot-like, with a prominent hooked nose and shiny bald skull, but any similarity ended there. He could call upon a vast store of professional knowledge and make it comprehensible to the layman in clear, unhesitating speech. He must have gauged the poverty of religious belief in the camp and decided to meet it head on.

He gave a short series of talks on religious topics, intentionally choosing those which could be regarded as controversial; the 'Blessed Trinity', for example. He suggested interpretations of the mysteries of Christian doctrine in practical terms and gave meaningful explanations of Christian philosophy. I would not go so far as to say that he converted the unbelievers, but there was no doubting the impact made on the large attentive audiences that came to listen in increasing numbers. There was no repetition of the slanging matches which had been the bitter experience of some chaplains. His talks provided food for thought, and one was left with a feeling of admiration and perhaps envy for the man himself, and concern for what he had to say.

* * *

The only other religious occasion of any importance at Padula was a pastoral visit from a high official of the Vatican. He brought sacred medallions for the Roman Catholics and a message of hope and the blessing from the Holy Father for everyone.

Chapter 11

Human Relations Under Strain

With the return to a more settled way of life, the strained atmosphere and uncertainties of personal relationships, so evident in the early days, gradually evaporated. No longer was the need felt for the close, constant companionship of just one or two people to the exclusion of others. Men now broke out of their insularity and were happy to seek the company of those with whom they had found something in common. Persons with similar vocational interests tended to be drawn together, as were those who regarded themselves as intellectuals.

As time passed, distinctions of rank and seniority became blurred, especially in the minds of juniors. It appeared almost irrelevant in a situation such as ours, where one and all had been reduced to the common status of PoW.

A common status we may have had, but it did not prevent the deeply rooted distinctions between social classes emerging, slowly but surely, and reasserting themselves. Yet, overriding all relationships, by far the strongest links were those already forged by the regimental system.

The regiment was the family, and family ties took precedence over others. The welfare and behaviour of one member was the concern of all. In no small way this spirit played an important part in the maintenance of discipline. There was an occasion, for example, when the SBO decided that it was high time all beards, other than naval, were removed. These facial growths were relics of earlier days, but now there was no excuse for anyone to remain unshaven. Some officers, either through vanity or laziness, had persisted in retaining their beards and were now reluctant to lose them. Eventually, everyone complied, except one officer who stubbornly refused. His stand, however, was short-lived. One evening he was escorted to the bathroom by his brother officers; thirty minutes later, he emerged clean shaven. Disgracing the regiment was the unpardonable sin.

The authority of the SBO was exercised and respected as in any other military unit, but he had no means of imposing punishment on offenders. This was the prerogative of the Italian camp commandant, who could award solitary confinement for a maximum of thirty days in the 'cooler'. But discipline was never a problem in our camp; life was orderly and peaceful, and I did not witness a single instance of a serious quarrel.

This harmony extended across the various components of the camp community, which included Indians, South Africans, Australians and New Zealanders, in addition to the British. The senior officer of each contingent was expected to impose his authority on his own countrymen whenever necessary, but all acknowledged the final word of the SBO. Naturally, there were times when national prejudice and suspicion were in evidence, but these usually took the form of light-hearted banter.

Between British and Indians there was genuine mutual trust and respect. Relations with men of the white Commonwealth, while much closer and equally cordial, were nevertheless seldom completely relaxed. They were jealous of their independence and acutely sensitive to any suggestion that they were beholden to the mother country or that we had any authority over their affairs. We used to joke that the Australian was such a well-balanced chap because he had a chip on both shoulders. We were, of course, all part of the Eighth Army and comrades in arms, but since the United Kingdom was the major contributor in terms of men and materials, we played a leading part and exercised overall command. This was inevitable, but remained a source of mild resentment.

The British tended to play this down, but there were times when a tactless remark made in mixed company caused offence. On the other hand, our Commonwealth colleagues seemed to have no qualms about openly criticising us and emphasising their superior standard of living. Boasting about their higher rates of Army pay was one sure way of putting us down.

Our common heritage of language and culture created such a vast area of contact that the occasional point of friction was to be expected. The important truth, however, was that we enjoyed a relationship of trust and understanding that was quite unique among free, independent nations. There were no foreigners among members of the Commonwealth.

Any minor differences, whether international or inter-service, were never displayed in front of our enemies. For them, we put on a bold front. We could be very noisy and boisterous at play, but the moment the bugle sounded for roll call, we regarded ourselves as on parade, and our bearing and behaviour were beyond reproach. Due respect was paid to rank, and military courtesies were exchanged in the normal way, not only between ourselves but also with the Italians. We were proud of our high standard of military discipline and glad to demonstrate it.

* * *

The small syndicates of two or three officers which had been formed early on proved to be conveniently sized units for sharing the odd chore, pooling items of food from Red Cross parcels, taking turns at brewing tea and sharing the cost of local newspapers. From the beginning I had been, more or less, in a syndicate with two other officers of the Welch, Bert Hyde and Louis Constable.

The three of us had at one time served together in the 18th Welch when stationed in the United Kingdom and had subsequently joined the 1st Welch in the Middle East, though at different times. Bert was the most recent arrival, having caught up with the battalion when in Benghazi. In fact, it was the day before Rommel's tanks rumbled into the city and took it over, and Bert found himself 'in the bag' in record quick time. We used to pull his leg that he had travelled non-stop from Newport to Naples.

Bert was the perfect companion in our circumstances. Older than Louis or myself, he had seen pre-war service as an NCO on the North-West Frontier of India and was now a commissioned quartermaster. He was short and wiry, with a Cockney sense of humour which never failed him, come what may. There was a twinkle in his sharp eyes, especially when waiting for the penny to drop after one of his puns or jokes. His chirpiness and rapid speech punctuated with Urdu expressions were a constant source of amusement to us. Bert was a generous man, particularly towards his friends. He was always neat and tidy and despised anyone who was otherwise.

Louis, by contrast, was somewhat lethargic. He was heavily built, though not tall, with a large square jaw and prominent white teeth. He

Desert training, Nile Delta, November 1941.
Ross was part of a contingent of over 200 sent
to Egypt to make good the losses suffered by
1 Welch following the German invasion of Crete.
(*Ross Family Archive*)

A boat load of Italians captured in the Western Desert on the way to the prison camps.

⊗ — Do you recognize me

Jimmy Day, prior to being captured himself, escorting Italian PoWs by boat in North Africa. Published
by an Egyptian newspaper. Jimmy is at the top of the photograph. He had positioned a soldier with
grenades in the crow's nest in case the Italians tried to take over the boat. (*Day Family Archive*)

The author's anti-tank company armed with similar 37mm Bofors Guns. In a defensive position 50 miles south of Benghazi, 1 Welch were part of the Eighth Army's front line. The Swedish Bofors was issued to the Eighth Army to replace the 2-pounders lost after the fall of France. It was to prove no match for Rommel's Panzers.

Padula Monastery PoW Camp, where Ross was held before being taken to Fontanellato. A UNESCO World Heritage Site, there had been a monastery there since 1306. It was also Garibaldi's base and an internment camp in the First World War.

Fontanellato PoW Camp was originally built as an orphanage. An anti-fascist town, its inhabitants gave considerable assistance to the PoWs during their mass escape after the Italian Armistice on 8 September 1943.

Lieutenant Jimmy Day MC, Welch Regt, in US Army uniform having reached US lines after the Italian Armistice. The Americans, seeing Day's ragged uniform, dressed him in one of theirs. (*Day Family Archive*)

The River Po, crossed by Ross and Day after their escape from Fontanellato. All the bridges were guarded, but an Italian, suspecting they were British PoWs, rowed them across under cover of darkness.

Como, where Ross and Day were recaptured in sight of Switzerland. Probably just as well as internment would have awaited them, along with over 1,000 British servicemen who were detained under the Geneva Convention until the end of the war. (*Ross Family Archive*)

Lieutenant George Bell, Highland Light Infantry. He and Ross escaped together after the Italian Armistice. A tea-planter from Ceylon, he was to return there after the war. (*Ross Family Archive*)

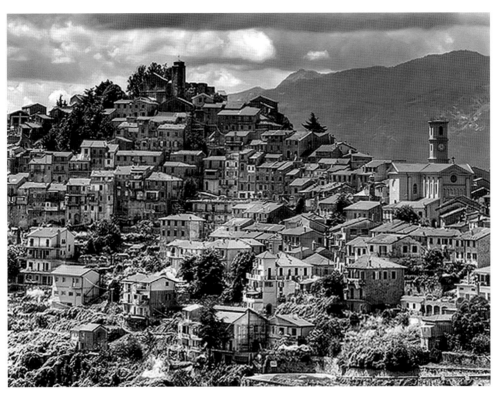

Baiardo, Liguria, a medieval village 3,000ft above sea level, the site of Ross and Bell's first encounter with partisans. They had hoped that Ross and Bell were SOE officers and would bring them weapons.

Stone huts near Baiardo, a partisan hideout, typical of their accommodation. Ross and Bell made it a rule never to sleep in the same place for more than one night consecutively. (*Ross Family Archive*)

Bordighera, Liguria, on the Italian Riviera, 20km from the French frontier. It contains a British War Cemetery built in 1918 for some of the British soldiers who had died in Italy during the First World War.

Villa Llo di Mare on the coast east of Bordighera, the home of the Porcheddu family, who would shelter Ross and Bell. (*Ross Family Archive*)

Beppe Porcheddu in 1922 using a walking stick as a result of his First World War injuries whilst an officer with 3rd Alpini Regiment fighting the Austrians and Germans. (*Ross Family Archive*)

Ross and Bell's successful hiding place in the villa. Even when the Fascists searched the house, it was never discovered. (*Ross Family Archive*)

Federico Assandria after miraculously surviving a German firing squad. He had tried to escape by boat to Corsica with Ross and Bell. After the war he emigrated to Venezuela, where he was to run a successful business. (*Ross Family Archive*)

Vincenzo Gismondi on the run in the Apennines after the discovery of the aborted attempt to row to Corsica. (*Ross Family Archive*)

Partisan commander 'Vittò' Guglielmo. Born San Remo 1916, fought in the International Brigade in the Spanish Civil War and commanded the partisan Garibaldi Division in Northern Italy. Interrogated Ross and Bell, who were suspected to be German spies. (*Copyright Alzani Editore*)

Lieutenant Ardell Klemme, USAF, B25 pilot, No 340 Group, 489 Squadron. He escaped by boat with Ross and Bell, reaching Monte Carlo on 16 March 1945. (*Copyright Gruppo Sbarchi Vallecrosia*)

Captain Robert Bentley MC in the Western Desert. A fluent Italian speaker, he was recruited by SOE and operated in Italy with the partisans and Ross and Bell. (*Bentley Family Archive*)

Hideout where Ross and Bell rejoined the partisan group after the Porcheddu family were forced to abandon the villa. (*Ross Family Archive*)

Partisans in the mountains in Liguria.

Partisans of Garibaldi Division, distinguishable by their red scarves. Communists, some of whom had gained operational experience fighting in the International Brigade in the Spanish Civil War. Ross and Bell were to join them.

Casa del Mattone, partisan house near the Porcheddu villa. Ross, Bell and partisans were to hide here after German and Fascist searches in the mountains. Ross and Bell escaped when the house was raided by Fascists and the partisans arrested. The house featured in Giovanni Antonio's novel *Il Dottor Antonio*, written to gain British support for Italian unification and responsible for considerable British interest in Bordighera, where many Britons were to settle. (*Ross Family Archive*)

The Porcheddu family in happier times. The Bordighera promenade was later named 'Lungomare Argentina' in honour of Eva Peron, who visited the town in 1947. (*Ross Family Archive*)

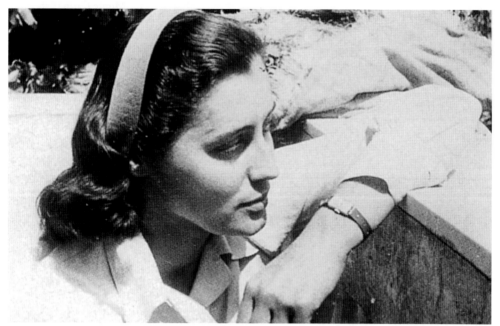

Giovanna. (*Ross Family Archive*)

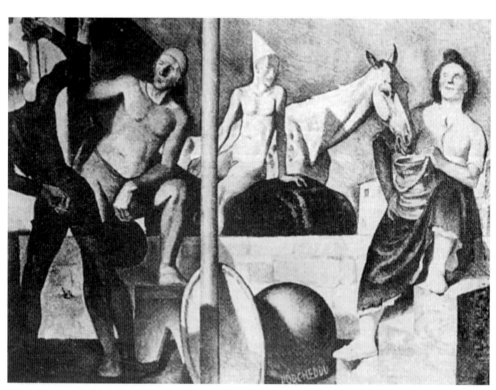

'Acrobats', watercolour on maple wood by Beppe Porcheddu, 1943. Beppe was to be acknowledged as one of Italy's greatest illustrators, knighted in 1925 by King Vittorio Emanuele III for his contribution to the arts. (*Ross Family Collection*)

Monte Carlo harbour, where Ross and Bell finally reached freedom. (*Ross Family Archive*)

Returning convoy and first sight of the UK through the damp morning fog of the Clyde estuary – the place from which, nearly four years earlier, Michael Ross had sailed out on a sunny autumn evening bound for North Africa. (*Ross Family Archive*)

Return to the Porcheddu Villa Llo di Mare after the war and reunion with the Porcheddu family. (*Ross Family Archive*)

Wedding of Michael and Giovanna in 1946. (*Ross Family Archive*)

Double wedding at Llo Di Mare, 11 October 1946, the author and Giovanna on the right and twin sister Ninilla and Captain Philip Garigue, Royal Fusiliers on the left. (*Ross Family Archive*)

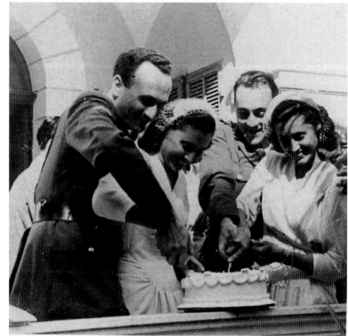

Honeymoon in Venice, October 1946.

Bordighera Memorial to partisans killed in the war. Renato Brunati's name heads the list. He was the first partisan that Ross and Bell encountered. (*Ross Family Archive*)

The author serving in Korea post-war. (*Ross Family Archive*)

The author and family in 1996 in Pen Bryn, Brecon, when his son, Brigadier David Ross, was commanding 160 (Wales) Brigade. The occasion was Michael and Giovanna's 50th wedding anniversary. (*Ross Family Archive*)

was a solid, stubborn individual but a thoroughly honest and dependable friend. He was a man with strong religious convictions, quite incorruptible and clearly suited to his peacetime profession of banking.

Bert, Louis and I got along well together, although, of the three I tended at times to be the odd man out. I could never commit myself wholly to friendships, at least not to the extent that these became apparent in prison camp early on, when some men were never out of each other's company and virtually shunned everyone else. I could never forego independence to that degree; I always needed an escape route.

No matter how confined and congested life may have been, each of us still retained our private worlds full of our thoughts and dreams for the future. The vital link with the reality of these worlds was the precious letter from home, or what was left of it after the censor in Rome had made his marks. But writing back from camp did not come easily. One had the same problem as the child at boarding school endeavouring to say something new in his regular letter home about an existence which the recipient could never really know or understand.

We were allowed to send one letter each week; they were, of course, strictly censored, too, before despatch. Mine alternated between my mother and my fiancée, as did those of Louis. Bert was already married with children, so his correspondence was concerned with his domestic responsibilities; they reflected a stable happy marriage and home.

Although both Louis and I were engaged to girls at home, there was a difference. His exchange of letters represented the straightforward continuation of a long friendship. The war had simply caused a postponement of their plans to marry, so when it was over they would take up their lives again where they had left off. It was all taken for granted. In my case, however, there was not the same firm base on which to build. I had met Margaret just a few short months before leaving England. It had been a first, innocent affair for both of us, and when I received orders to proceed overseas I felt I should acknowledge my sincerity by asking her to marry me, and she accepted.

Now, for the first time, I started to analyse the full implications of what I had done. I had the nagging feeling that I had been unfair to her. She was a very attractive girl, still in her teens, and exposed to the highly emotional social atmosphere of a country at war. I told myself that it had been wrong to commit her in this way; the more so in my present position, where the prospect of an early reunion was remote. Right now, with the crucial battles still to come, there seemed no end in sight to this war. It could be a long haul, and prisoners like ourselves would not see their homeland again until it was all over. I argued with myself that it would not be reasonable to expect a relationship based on a few months' acquaintance to withstand the strains of separation through so many difficult years ahead. Finally, I sought the opinion of a wise, understanding friend – he was also a lawyer.

'You've certainly put the onus on the girl, old chap,' was his only comment.

That decided me. I took courage and wrote to Margaret explaining how I felt. But I realized much later that I had been cowardly, for instead of making a clean break I gave her the option, and she would have none of it! It might have seemed to her that I was looking for reassurance, or possibly she thought that it was simply a case of depression and I was being magnanimous. Neither was true. Deep down I had started having doubts about myself. We did not broach the subject again, and our letters continued in the old vein as if nothing had happened.

Shortly afterwards, I received a new portrait of Margaret which I hung on the wall above my bed. An Australian passing by, to whom I had never spoken before, came over to peer closely at it. He grinned and said, 'Best looking gal in camp so far.'

Chapter 12

Escapes and the Aftermath

The bugle call for muster parade had sounded at an unusually early hour. It was four in the morning and still dark. Guards suddenly appeared in the dormitories running around ordering us from our beds and ushering us down to the courtyard below. Slowly, companies of bleary-eyed prisoners formed up in their usual places for roll call along the length of one of the cloisters. The entire Italian staff seemed to be on duty, and when everyone was in place, the commandant himself appeared, serious-faced. It had happened, as it was bound to sooner or later – there had been an escape.

The process of checking names, of counting and recounting, went on and on so long that the dawn was well advanced before we were finally dismissed. We were not allowed back in our quarters, however, as an intensive search of the accommodation was under way. Cupboards were ransacked, items of food that were found were confiscated along with our home-made cookers and utensils used for brewing up in the evenings. The Italians were furious, understandably so, as the check had confirmed that ten prisoners were missing. A tunnel had been discovered leading out from below the stone floor of one of the downstairs rooms.

During the next few days there was a succession of long and frequent roll calls – one way of inflicting mild collective punishment. Reprisals also took the form of the imposition of certain restrictions. The paddock was placed out of bounds, the privilege of organized walks for small parties of prisoners outside camp under armed escort was withdrawn and activities such as the drama group were terminated. The latter, partly because of its use of civilian clothes for plays, had been exploited by escapees.

These losses were compensated for by the satisfaction we derived, when on parade for roll call, of watching the anxious faces of our captors as they laboriously checked and rechecked their lists. We had humiliated our enemies and in doing so had restored just a little of our pride.

Unfortunately, it was short-lived. Within days, all ten who had escaped were apprehended and returned to camp; but it had been worth it. As for the staff themselves, there were wholesale sackings on orders from Rome, including that of the decent commandant, who was replaced by an obnoxious and pompous Carabinieri colonel.

These events shook the camp out of its lethargy. Up to that point we had settled down to a comfortable routine existence, partaking of outdoor sports and indoor recreational activities and relaxing in the enjoyment of an ever expanding library. It had brought a sharp reminder to everyone of the Army's standing order that the duty of every soldier taken prisoner is to make his escape whenever possible.

This first attempt at escape from Padula met with a mixed reception from the inmates. Some considered the ten to be heroes, but there were others who raised their voices in dissent, complaining about the 'selfishness' of those whose useless actions had achieved nothing and only made life less tolerable for everyone. But secretly there was envy of those few who had successfully broken out of the camp and who could now lay claim to the prestigious label of 'escapee'.

To make a successful escape was the crowning ambition of every prisoner, as it would be a complete vindication of his surrender. Some men were obsessed with the idea of escaping from the day they were captured, but the majority hardly gave it a serious thought. It was not that they had no wish to escape, rather that they regarded the problems involved as virtually insurmountable and so resigned themselves to seeing the war out as PoWs.

It must be said that the opportunities for escape were few and far between. The security in Italian PoW camps was extremely tight and the physical defences around camps quite formidable. The Italians had an outstanding record in the holding of prisoners. At this point in time, with many thousands behind barbed wire, only one officer was known to have succeeded in escaping and reaching freedom.

Whenever a break was made it usually exposed some weakness in the camp's security which the authorities were quick to rectify. It also induced them to review and strengthen camp security in general. Furthermore, an escape invariably brought in its wake a series of restrictions and curtailment of privileges for the camp as a whole. It was therefore not something to be undertaken lightly. Acts of bravado helped no one. Breaking out was all very well, but the problem of getting clear of enemy territory required careful thought and preparation and this was all too often neglected.

It was therefore important to exercise control on all such activities, in order to ensure that ill-conceived attempts at escape did not jeopardize the plans of others who might be better equipped but were perhaps taking longer over their preparations. For this reason, escape committees existed in all camps, presided over by a senior officer appointed by the SBO.

Their task was to vet all plans of escape and, if approved, render all possible help. By this means, worthy schemes could be assisted and properly co-ordinated, while foolhardy ones could be scotched in time. A very serious view was taken of any attempt at escape without the prior consent of the escape committee.

* * *

There was one further attempt at escape from Padula. Some months later, four officers dressed in Italian uniforms which they had somehow managed to acquire made their way secretly into the guards' compound and attempted to pass out through the main gates by mingling with the soldiery during their general exodus at the end of the day's duties. Unfortunately, a sharp-eyed NCO on gate duty recognized one of them and raised the alarm; all four were caught on the spot.

This attempt at escape had an unpleasant aftermath. During the usual ransacking of the escapees' rooms, the authorities discovered a notebook containing a detailed appreciation of the camp's security measures linked with advice on ways and means of defeating them. It was a complete handbook for the would-be escapee and an equally valuable document for the enemy. It had been the work of one of the four and should have been properly safeguarded.

That evening, the SBO, Brigadier Mountain, addressed the whole camp in the dining hall on the seriousness of what had happened and warned that the officer concerned would be court-martialled after the war. We did not see the four again, since they were despatched to Camp

Garvi in the north. This was a fortress-like place to which escapees were sent on recapture. Its security was reckoned to be a match for anyone with ideas of getting out.

While we did not exactly envy these four being sent to a top security prison, they were at least experiencing a change of scene, and that was something most prisoners would have jumped at, just for its own sake. I certainly felt that way.

There had, in fact, been a few relocations from Padula at various times. The first to leave were severely wounded men, reputedly for repatriation; then all Indian prisoners had been taken out and despatched to an exclusively Indian camp – a blessing for them, no doubt, in terms of catering. Later, all of the very senior officers were transferred to a small camp specially set up for them – this met with popular acclaim from all sides. Finally, our naval colleagues, much to their delight, were reassigned to a camp elsewhere run by the Italian navy – they were probably anticipating special treatment from their maritime brethren.

Witnessing all these departures was like seeing friends off on holiday while you remained behind; I found it rather depressing. But then one morning, unexpectedly, everything suddenly changed for me too.

A list of fifteen names appeared on the notice board under the heading 'Immediate transfers to Fontanellato', and mine was among them. The tip of my tongue froze, I was overjoyed, I felt as if I had been given a new lease of life. The fact that I was simply exchanging one prison camp for another was unimportant just then; I was moving on, and that meant everything.

No reason for the posting had been given, nor did we know the basis on which this small group had been chosen from the several hundred men in camp. We were a mixed bunch. I was the only Welch officer so, regretfully, I would be parting from old friends; at the same time, I would be breaking ties and, to be honest, this could be refreshing.

But there was another new, important consideration. Recently, there had been a complete reversal of fortunes in North Africa. Montgomery had been victorious at El Alamein – the news was greeted with spontaneous cheering around the camp – and now the enemy was in full retreat. At long last there was a real prospect of an invasion of mainland Italy, and the odds were therefore on the southern parts being liberated first. Fontanellato, we were soon to learn, was way up in the north, so the thought of deserting Padula at this time caused some misgivings among those about to leave. For my part, I was more than happy to make the move; I was eager to go, taking comfort from the maxim that in war the unexpected can always happen.

* * *

With the prospect of departure from Padula to start a new life elsewhere, I looked back and reflected on the consequences of nearly a year's confinement. Above all was the sad realization that it had been an appalling waste of one's youth; there was just nothing to show for it. Looking ahead, the thought of further empty years was daunting.

Yet outwardly, I don't think we had changed much; high spirits and good humour were still frequently in evidence, while cases of serious depression were few. Physically, we were all in remarkably good shape, despite a general loss of weight, or possibly because of it. Hunger, though, had revealed men's weaknesses and their shameless greed as nothing else could. Regardless of social status or upbringing, breaches of good manners and lack of personal restraint were commonplace whenever food was at stake.

Being deprived of outside contacts, particularly with members of the opposite sex, had not, I suspect, had an important bearing on our lives. Men, more so than women, perhaps, can readily find satisfaction and fulfilment in their own company. Contrary to what one might have expected, interest in sex seemed to have diminished; the subject did not figure much in our conversation, so presumably it did not occupy our thoughts much either. Possibly the established practice in the officers' mess of never broaching the subject of women was still holding good. It was the topic of food that seemed to supersede everything, and I must admit that when contemplating my impending move to a new camp, this was uppermost in my mind.

THE WAR OFFICE,
CAS. P.W.,
CURZON STREET HOUSE,
CURZON STREET,
LONDON, W.1.

OS/2010/R. (Cas. P.W.)

Your Reference

30th July, 1943.

Madam,

    I am directed to acknowledge receipt of your letter of 19th
July, and to state that Camp 49, P.M. 3200, is situated at Reggio
Nele, Emilea, Italy, but it must be remembered that place names
must not be quoted when addressing correspondence to Captain Ross.

    Bomber Command are kept fully informed of localities of all
our prisoner of war camps.

    With reference to your enquiry regarding your son's kit,
information has just been received which indicates that it has
now arrived in this country and is stored with Messrs. Cox and
King's (Agents) Limited.

    You will no doubt appreciate that the Department is normally
precluded from authorising the disposal of an officer's kit
except on his personal instructions but if you wish to claim the
kit and have in your possession any letter or document from
Captain Ross in which his wishes regarding the disposal of his
possessions are indicated, the Department would be prepared to
issue the necessary instructions for the release of the kit on
receipt of a copy of the letter or document or its relevant extract.

    Any communication sent would, of course, be returned to you
in due course.

    Would you be good enough to state to which address you
desire future communications to be sent.

          I am, Madam,
          Your obedient Servant,

Mrs. M.R. Ross,
   179, Stanwell Road,
     Penarth,
       Glamorganshire.

MoD letter to Michael's mother concerning her son's kit following capture. (*Ross Family Archive*)

Chapter 13

A Taste of Freedom in Northern Italy

T he train journey north was exhilarating. It felt good to be in contact once again with the life and movement of the outside world. We travelled up through the mountainous backbone of Italy until we emerged on to the flat plain of Lombardy to reach our destination, the town of Fontanellato.

Our new home turned out to be a recently constructed children's orphanage, hurriedly converted into a prisoner of war camp for 250 officers. It was a four-storey, red brick building situated on a fairly busy thoroughfare, a striking contrast to the ancient, isolated, stone-built monastery of Padula.

The accommodation itself can only be described as princely. There were spacious dormitories with marble floors, modern kitchens and refectory, numerous bathrooms complete with mirrors and showers, an assembly room with a stage and, for our spiritual needs, a beautiful chapel with stained-glass windows. If PoW camps had been graded, this one would have been 'five-star'.

As for the food, it could not have been better. Located, as we were, on the fringe of a vast food-producing area, we benefited from a plentiful supply. Not only that, but we also enjoyed a well-balanced diet with imaginative menus thanks to our being able to consign the food from our Red Cross parcels directly to the kitchens, something undreamed of before. The days when these eagerly awaited parcels were clawed open and their contents carefully apportioned under the scrutiny of staring hungry eyes were a thing of the past.

On Sundays, the inhabitants of the surrounding countryside would converge on the town and there would be a continuous procession of predominantly young girls along the road outside. They were curious to get a glimpse of us and, naturally, we were more than pleased to see them. It was a novel situation for us after the monastic existence of Padula.

Yet this incursion of a new dimension into our lives was unsettling; it disturbed the equilibrium of a well-ordered male community.

However, these delights, remote as they were, were soon curtailed. We were forbidden to stand near the windows facing the road under pain of being shot at by the sentries outside. In due course, the odd hole in the upstairs ceilings, caused by shots from down below, bore witness to the temptation to flout this tiresome restriction. There were some near misses, but fortunately no casualties.

The majority of officers in Fontanellato had come from two old camps at Sulmona and Chieti. Many of them were regulars who had been serving in the pre-war Middle East garrisons and had been captured in the early desert campaigns. With the prospect of being prisoners for the duration, they feared their military careers were over. They could not help feeling depressed as younger, non-regular officers with newly-acquired senior ranks started to arrive. A regular lieutenant of infantry, who had been 'in the bag' for two years, was watching the arrival of a new batch of prisoners one day. Suddenly he exclaimed, 'Hell, there's my batman; he's been commissioned!' He had also been promoted to captain.

PoW Food Coupon for purchases from the camp shop. (*Ross Family Archive*)

Rank in a PoW camp carried prestige and was accorded privileges, albeit limited ones, as in any other service unit. Our topsy-turvy situation, although unavoidable, was none the less demoralizing. Junior naval officers had some compensation as they received automatic promotion through two ranks, while junior RAF officers acquired one promotion on a time basis in the same way. Army officers, however, retained the rank they had on capture for the duration of their imprisonment.

* * *

It was among the ex-Sulmona group that I discovered another officer of the Welch Regiment, Jimmy Day. His name was known to me, but we had never met before. He was serving with the 1st battalion in Crete well before my time and was one of those left behind when German paratroops invaded the island and forced the British to evacuate. However, before everyone was rounded up, Jimmy, with some others, seized a motor boat and headed for the North African coast. They almost made it before running out of fuel. Jimmy then detached a dinghy and rowed to the shore, but unluckily he landed in enemy territory and was captured. Those in the stranded motor boat were more fortunate; thanks to a favourable current, they drifted eastwards and came ashore on our side of the line.

Jimmy was a solitary man who walked about the camp with downcast eyes and springy step. He had a lean figure, prominent nose, small mouth with a large gap in his front teeth, a short beard and a mop of sandy hair standing on end. He wore a fixed puzzled expression which, I very soon learned, reflected his constant mental struggle with the problem of how to get out. The idea of escaping had become an obsession.

Being the only officers of the Welch in that camp, we naturally got together. It was not long, of course, before we were seriously exploring the possibilities of escaping. Jimmy had a positive approach and plenty of ideas but was somewhat oblivious of the pitfalls. We discussed the subject ad nauseam; our deliberations usually terminated with my trying to convince him that his various schemes would end in disaster. It was like playing skittles; Jimmy would set them up and I would knock them down.

But we pursued our intentions urgently for one very good reason. Fontanellato was a new camp, not built as a prison, and its security had never been put to the test. Such weaknesses as there might be would in time be recognized by the authorities or exposed by future escape attempts, and duly eliminated. Most likely there were other prisoners thinking along the same lines and secretly planning to escape while the going was good. Therefore the sooner we were able to devise a plan acceptable to the committee, the better.

* * *

After much discussion we finally succeeded in agreeing on a definite plan. It would involve considerable preparatory work, but the basic idea was simple. Yet it was so unconventional that we reckoned that, if everything went well beforehand, we could get away with it.

This, then, was the situation. Adjacent to the rear of the camp building was a rectangular field, the size of a small football pitch, enclosed by a high wire fence. It lay just outside the main perimeter fence which encircled the whole camp. Between this perimeter fence and the building itself was a long narrow compound where we could exercise and where we were required to assemble for roll calls.

There was a security gate in the main perimeter fence which gave immediate access to the field directly from the compound, and after morning roll call it was opened to allow us into the field for the day.

At six o'clock in the evening the field was cleared and prisoners were moved back into the inner compound, where we were paraded and counted again. Meanwhile, half a dozen guards would make an inspection of the empty field, before finally withdrawing and locking the gate for the night.

At each corner of the field was an elevated watchtower. The two at the further end were manned only when the field was in use but the two nearest ones were manned night and day as they were sited on the main perimeter fence surrounding the camp. At night this perimeter fence was brightly floodlit, while the fencing of the other three sides of the field at the back was left in darkness.

It was not difficult to conclude from all this that anyone who succeeded in concealing himself below ground in the field during the day, and remained hidden there until it was dark, could then emerge, crawl under the unlit part of the wire fence at the end of the field and make off. It would, of course, be essential for his absence on the six o'clock roll call to be covered up, but that would be the least of the problems. Jimmy and I started to formulate our plans on this scenario.

The basic idea was simple enough, but there were serious practical problems. How do we dig a trench in hard ground without some tools and cover it over without arousing the suspicions of the guards who were always prowling around? How do we bury ourselves in such a way that we could survive the four or five hours' wait until dark? In addition, the finished job would have to be good enough to escape the notice of the sentries inspecting the field at the end of the day when everyone had left. We could see no satisfactory way of overcoming these difficulties, and had almost resigned ourselves to giving up the idea altogether, when quite unexpectedly the authorities unwittingly provided the perfect solution.

* * *

Now it happened that the surface of the field was very rough and uneven, with numerous small hummocks, so the Italians were asked if it could be levelled off to make it suitable for ball games. For their part, they were only too pleased to oblige; playing games would keep us healthy and happy and divert our attention and energies from vexatious occupations like trying to escape.

True to their word, within a few days, a consignment of picks and shovels arrived and we were told to get on with it. We could hardly believe our good fortune. Not only did we have the tools for the job presented to us officially and exactly where we wanted them, but we could now set to work on our project under the guise of carrying out legitimate field works.

We seized the opportunity to present our ready-made plans to the escape committee straight away. They seemed quite impressed and promised to lend their full support. There were still some loose ends to be tied up, and they proposed a further meeting a few days later.

At the second meeting we were told that three other officers had come forward with plans similar to ours, and that whilst Jimmy and myself should have priority, it was suggested that the five of us combine our efforts. We were mildly disappointed to learn that someone else had hit on the same idea and only hoped it had not occurred to the Italians as well. Nevertheless, we were quite glad to have help, as there was a lot of preliminary work to be done in a short space of time. Fortunately, the newcomers were steady types whose involvement could only be an asset.

Our new collaborators were Tony Roncoroni, Peter Jocelyn and Toby Graham. Tony was a swarthy, handsome man, capped several times for England at rugger. He was the biggest man in the camp and the most popular. Peter was short, ungainly, had delicate white hands, was softly spoken and an introvert. He had spent his pre-war years in the Argentine in the unlikely role of cattle rancher. His mild manner disguised a tough core and, according to some, an iron nerve. The third newcomer, Toby, was a tall fair-haired youth with aquiline features and limpid blue eyes. He was a regular gunner officer whose future career, he was convinced, had been undermined by his capture and imprisonment so early in the war. A successful escape might put things right for him.

The five of us got together and quickly drew up our plans in detail. Speed was essential, as there was no knowing when the authorities might conclude that the field works had progressed sufficiently and withdraw the tools.

What was needed was a covered trench somewhere in the middle of the field in which we could remain concealed for some hours. Completion would likely take several days, but the moment the trench was long enough to take two, it was agreed that Jimmy and I should go. If all went well, the trench would be extended the next day to enable the other three to follow on.

We should have to contend with the vigilance of the sentries perched high up on the four-corner elevated watchtowers overlooking the field, as well as the attentions of a couple of prowler guards continuously moving around the field when it was occupied by prisoners.

It was clear that the trench would have to be as shallow as possible, about a foot; a deeper hole than this might be conspicuous and attract attention. For the roofing we would use bed boards. These were narrow planks, about 3ft long, which could be laid across the hole and covered with soil. It would mean limiting the width of the trench to 2ft, but we should be able to extend it for as long as necessary to accommodate us lying head to toe in a straight line.

We set to work cautiously in relays. After cutting the first few feet, a wooden board, taken from a bunk in the dormitory, was placed across the hole and covered with soil, thus concealing everything completely. The hole was then extended bit by bit while new boards were laid in position and immediately covered over in the same way. Thus there was never more than a narrow slit exposed at any time. If any of the guards wandered dangerously close to our site, we had several ploys for directing their interest and steps elsewhere. Even the vast majority of the prisoners themselves, we reckoned, were unaware of what was going on. Knowledge of our scheme had been kept on a strictly 'need to know' basis.

We were fortunate to have the bed boards; they proved ideal for the job and could be easily carried from the main building hidden inside folded deckchairs. Chairs were constantly being taken in and out of the field by individuals anyway.

* * *

After four days' work the trench was almost long enough to hold two; by the following day it would certainly be ready and, as prearranged, Jimmy and I were to get in first. Once we were underground, our colleagues would ensure that the entrance hole was closed up and concealed. We, in turn, would cover up the hole after emerging that night and, hopefully, leave no trace of our departure. Provided our absence remained undetected, then work could proceed normally the following day on extending the trench to enable the other three to make their escape that night in the same manner.

So far, everything had gone remarkably smoothly without a single hitch or anxious moment. This led some to suspect that the Italians were already fully aware of what we were up to. It was suggested that they were intentionally allowing us to go ahead and dig our own grave, then going to make an example of us when they caught us red-handed. We shrugged off any such ideas; somehow that sort of scheming did not seem in keeping with the Italian character.

* * *

Apart from our work in the field, preparations had been going on behind the scenes, directed by the committee. Getting clear of the camp was only a first hurdle; there remained the problem of covering 100 miles of enemy territory undetected and, finally, crossing a guarded frontier into Switzerland.

Our intention was to move by night and hide by day, keeping clear of people and avoiding towns and roads. In the event of our being challenged, our cover story was that we were German civilian workers at the Fiat works in Turin on a short walking holiday. To back this up, we were provided with exact copies of the identity cards carried by this category of worker. Produced by a skilled draughtsman with the help of an officer of the Intelligence Corps, they were little masterpieces. The lettering was so perfect it could have been done by machine. To provide our photographs, glossy magazines had been searched for likenesses, which were then cut out and embossed on the cards.

We were told that in the event of capture we were to do everything possible to prevent these cards getting into enemy hands. As the chances of being caught were greatest in the precincts of the camp itself, we were told to tape them to the soles of our feet before leaving, so that if we were caught and stripped, the cards might remain undiscovered. Once clear of the vicinity of the camp, we could then carry them in the normal way.

Suitable clothes were no problem; white shirts with borrowed Air Force blue trousers gave the necessary civilian appearance. Hidden under loose-fitting pullovers were cloth belts each fitted with pockets holding eight flat cocoa tins filled with a mixture of chocolate, raisins, biscuits and Oxo – a doctor's recipe prepared in the kitchens. We counted on eating one a day, which should see us to the frontier. Forged letters addressed to our place of work from our imaginary girlfriends in Bremen, a hand-drawn map, compass, penknife, razor and a little local currency completed our equipment.

Finally, there were the roll calls to contend with. The committee were confident of being able to cover up our absence for forty-eight hours. This would give sufficient time for the three colleagues following in our footsteps the next day to get clear of the camp, before the fact of our disappearance was discovered.

Muster parades for officers were normally held each morning and evening in the compound adjacent to the field; at night, a head count was taken when everyone was in bed. Making good any deficiencies in the latter could easily be managed by the use of dummies, but deceiving the muster parades was more complicated and involved a variety of stratagems.

The sick list, for example, could be manipulated; an officer checked as 'sick in bed' by the Italian duty officer doing his rounds would later scamper along unguarded corridors and staircases and be counted as someone else 'sick' in another part of the building. Another trick would be to arrange for an other rank, who was supposedly on a working party, to be smuggled into the officers' muster parade as substitute for a missing officer.

Of course, discrepancies would come to light if the authorities conducted a hundred per cent physical check by name of all officers and other ranks together, but that was a lengthy business and done only occasionally. Hopefully, they would not choose to do so on the evening when we were lying underground. If they did, things could be messy and our chances of getting away would be pretty slim.

With the trench almost ready, a message came from the colonel of the escape committee: 'Ross and Day are to go tomorrow.' That evening, we observed the guards closely as they entered the field after it had been cleared. They collected and counted the tools and proceeded to search the ground, occasionally prodding it as they wandered about. We watched as they approached the vicinity of our carefully concealed trench but, as on previous occasions, nothing was discovered and the guards withdrew. Jimmy and I joked about it being the last time we would look out on to this scene. Tomorrow was to be our big day.

The next morning, Friday, 7 May 1943, was bright and clear. Normally, a stormy night with rain provided the ideal conditions for escape, as visibility for sentries was poor and they would be tempted to take shelter; besides which, unusual noises could go unheard. In our case, however, having to lie outside for nearly five hours in a shallow trench, a torrential downpour could spell disaster. But we had no need for concern; the sunny weather persisted throughout the day, and the final stages of our digging continued uninterrupted. By afternoon the trench was completed, on schedule and amply long enough to take the two of us.

We planned on entering the hole about 5.30 in the afternoon, giving us plenty of time to settle in and have the entrance well sealed before the deadline at six o'clock. I was to go in head first, turn on my back and scramble to the far end, to be followed by Jimmy, who would go in feet first. The narrow entrance above his head would then be boarded over and covered with earth, leaving us lying on our backs completely concealed below ground.

* * *

At four o'clock a substantial meal was smuggled up to our room, but we had little appetite and soon made our way down to the field. A variety of activities, intended as distractions for the sentries, were under way. A game of rugger had started, and an altercation between a few of the players, intended to hold the attention of the guards, was scheduled to occur at the crucial moment of our entry into the trench.

By 5.30 I was poised, kneeling on the ground, staring at the hole which had been opened up, awaiting my cue. Four men sitting casually nearby, each with an eye on a different sentry, were muttering continuously, 'Yes' or 'No', depending on whether or not their sentry was looking in our direction. The moment I got a simultaneous 'All clear!', I was to dive into the hole.

A rugger scrum came conveniently close to unsight the sentries on one side of the field. The seconds ticked by and then the awaited signal came; I went in head first. Unfortunately, we had misjudged the size of the opening needed and I got stuck half way in. An extra board was hastily removed, enabling me to turn on my back and edge my way, caterpillar-like, to the far end of the trench. I then lay still.

Inside it was pitch black in contrast to the brightness outside; there was no room to move and I could lift my head only an inch or so. For the first time in my life I experienced the shock of claustrophobia; my nerves were taut and I fought hard against panic. I think it must have been the voice of Joss outside saying, 'Are you all right Mike?' which brought me to my senses. Gradually, as my eyes adjusted, I could see a faint speck of light coming through the boards and earth above my head. I asked Joss if he could shift one of the clods of earth little to widen this crevice and provide more air as I had a feeling I was suffocating. We each had, in fact, a short piece of rubber tubing fixed through the board above our faces from which we could suck fresh air if needed. A few moments later, I could hear Jimmy scrambling in at the far end, after which the entrance was closed and covered over.

Underground, we were still able to hear the voices around us, and when the six o'clock whistle was blown, which was the signal to clear the field, we heard it quite distinctly. Our friends came close and mumbled, 'Cheerio, good luck', while the noises above gradually died away as the field emptied.

* * *

Before long, the guards entered the field to conduct their routine search. They were calling to each other as they spread out to comb the area. Suddenly I felt a heavy footfall immediately above my head; the boards creaked as dust fell on my mouth. I slid my hands up to my face for protection as I thought the roof was caving in. This individual had chosen to halt directly over the trench and was exchanging words with one of his colleagues. I could even hear his heavy breathing between words. Unfortunately, I could not make out what he was saying.

Much to my relief, he moved on, but it was disquieting to think that someone had approached and actually stopped on the exact place where we were hiding. I convinced myself that it was pure coincidence. But then a second unusual incident occurred. We heard the guards withdrawing from the field, having presumably completed their inspection; yet after a short interval they came back again. This was not normal and it puzzled us. However, they did not remain long; shortly afterwards they left and everything was silent again.

It was a while before Jimmy and I dared whisper to each other, reassuring ourselves that all was well. Nevertheless, the thought of that one guard and of the second visit to the field remained with me. The warnings, previously sounded, about the Italians having full knowledge of our venture, naturally came to mind again.

* * *

Arrangements had been made for a concert party to be held that evening in one of the dormitories facing the field. The usual boisterous noises might help divert the attention of the sentries from what would be happening in the field behind them. Part of the entertainment was to include a blast from a hunting horn at nine o'clock, the real object of which was to signal us that all was well.

I had anticipated that lying buried like this, in such cramped conditions, would be the longest five hours of my life, but it was not so. We joked that, perhaps like hibernating animals, our metabolism had slowed down. Anyway, the audible half-hour chimes of the clock, high above the main building, seemed to come and go remarkably quickly, and I felt almost relaxed as we came to the last thirty minutes of our vigil. Earlier on, I had watched the tiny speck of daylight through the crack above my head grow dimmer until it disappeared altogether.

We listened carefully for the tally-ho due at 9.00 but heard nothing, nor did we catch any sound of the concert party itself. But we were not unduly perturbed. Needless to say, having committed ourselves this far, nothing was going to divert us from our course now.

* * *

When it was past ten o'clock, with darkness well advanced, Jimmy made his move. Light crept into the trench as he removed the end boards. He heaved himself out silently and disappeared. I edged myself along the trench, feet first, to reach the opening. After something of a struggle, twisting and turning, I finally freed myself from the hole and lay flat on the ground outside, face downwards.

I was immediately startled and somewhat alarmed by the unexpected profusion of light everywhere. The surrounding countryside was blacked out, leaving the main building looking like some giant ocean liner at sea by night. Every window was illuminated and the outside walls were ablaze with beams from the perimeter arc lamps. I could see the sentries so clearly, perched on their watchtowers barely 30yds away. I felt vulnerable and exposed lying there in the reflected glow from all of this. I had blackened my face with soil while waiting in the trench but I doubted that this would afford much protection if a sentry happened to look in my direction.

I was desperate to get away quickly to the obscurity of the darkness at the far end of the field, but first I had to cover over the hole with the boards and soil to ensure it was not discovered in the morning. The chances of the other three following on the next day depended on it. Instinctively, I moved slowly, not wishing to attract the attention of the sentries. While endeavouring to perform this task conscientiously, I found it difficult to keep my eyes from focusing on the figures of the sentries silhouetted sharply against the brightly lit walls.

I had completed the work and was about to leave when, unexpectedly, I was forced to freeze. A lorry with its headlights full on had at that moment entered the side of the compound. It was veering around, with its beams sweeping across the field and coming towards me. I watched anxiously as the lights came nearer and nearer, until suddenly they were upon me. I buried my face in the ground, expecting the lights to pass over me. Instead, the vehicle halted, still pointing in my direction. My limbs were rigid, while my heart was pounding. I muttered a curse and a prayer between my teeth and, as if in response, the engine was switched off and the headlamps dimmed. If a sentry had, by chance, been looking my way at that split second he could not have failed to see me. But there was no reaction, no shots or searchlights were aimed at me, and I realized, gratefully, that the danger had passed.

* * *

I set off immediately, crawling crab-like over the ground with as much speed as I dared, to the appointed place at the wire near the bottom of the field. When I arrived I heard Jimmy's muted voice on the other side of the fence indicating the way through. He had cut, as pre-arranged, a couple of strands of wire to facilitate our passage. As I negotiated this obstacle, I bent the wires back in an attempt to hide any traces of our exit.

At last I emerged on the other side of the fence and went over to where Jimmy was crouching under a row of vines. We grasped each other by the hand, glanced momentarily at the lighted camp building for the last time and with unimaginable joy turned our backs on it and set off.

Those thrilling first moments of freedom are something I will never forget. It seemed that the world had suddenly opened up before me, and I felt intoxicated by the thought that I could now walk on and on as far as I wished, free of escorts and barriers. I recall being struck, at that moment, by the sheer simplicity of our transition from imprisonment to liberty; it had all been so easy, yet from behind bars the problems had seemed insurmountable.

* * *

We had planned on making an all-out effort to put as great a distance as possible between ourselves and the camp during that first night, before the light of day forced us to hide. It was our rule that we would travel only during the hours of darkness and stay put by day. In so doing, we would minimize the chances of being seen or spoken to.

Fontanellato was on the lower fringe of the great fertile plain of Lombardy, and since our route was northwards to Switzerland, we would have to cross the whole of this vast cultivated area. We very soon encountered the hazards of moving over this type of country. It was criss-crossed by elevated paths, sunken water courses and dykes, while in between there was row upon row of vine fencing and suchlike. It was intensive farming in the extreme. Furthermore, the relatively small size of holdings on this rich arable land meant that one could never get entirely clear of farmhouses and, as we were soon to discover, they all kept dogs.

It was frustrating trying to keep a straight course in these conditions, and we found ourselves constantly diverted by obstacles. On one such occasion early that night, Jimmy was trying to negotiate a narrow weir, lost his balance and slipped into the shallow water. But we could not let up for a moment and pressed on hard for about an hour, by which time we reckoned we had covered some four or five miles. We were already beginning to feel a little safer and so dropped down under a hedgerow for a short rest and to get our breath back.

(The Estate of Ian English)

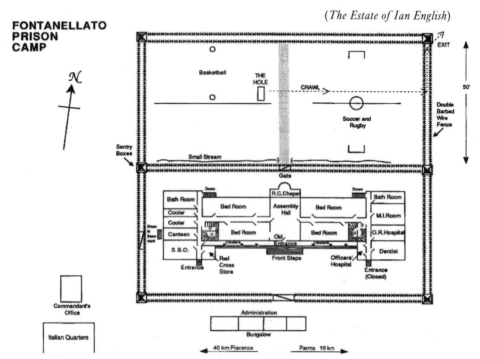

We removed our boots and stockings to recover the passes attached to the soles of our feet. To our dismay, Jimmy discovered that his precious document had already been churned into papier mâché – obviously a casualty of his little accident on the weir, although at the time we had not given it a thought. In silence, Jimmy squeezed out the remnants of his pass enmeshed in his sodden woollen stockings; it was clear not a scrap of it could be salvaged. It was a disastrous start and a serious loss in a country where so much importance was given to '*documenti*'.

* * *

The rest of the night passed uneventfully, but progress was disappointingly slow. We encountered the odd peasant but always chose to ignore them. If we were greeted, we responded with a muffled '*Sera*' and left it at that. At first light, we sought a place to hide.

Ideally, we needed somewhere that offered concealment, was located away from footpaths and preferably had access to drinking water. In our present surroundings such a combination would not be easy to find. However, on this first occasion we were lucky. We came across a thicket, away from a cultivated area, where there was little likelihood of encountering workers during the day; there was also the bonus of a tiny stream nearby. But equally important, there was shade. We were soon to realize that this was an essential adjunct to any hiding place under these cloudless Italian skies. Fifteen hours' exposure to sun would be killing.

We dropped into a daily routine: removal of boots to rest our feet, half a tin each of our rations, a drink of water and then an hour's sleep in turns while one kept watch. But prolonged sleep was difficult because of the discomfort of the hard ground, while hour after hour of the hot sun made us exceptionally thirsty. On this occasion, the trickle of water which had provided such a welcome morning drink had, to our dismay, completely dried up by midday.

* * *

At sundown we were ready and anxious to be on our way again. We estimated that although we had probably walked some 30 miles the previous night, we were likely to be still only about half that distance from Fontanellato, such was the winding and twisting of our trail. We already felt footsore as we set off. Our feet had gone soft from the constant wearing of plimsolls in camp, despite some limited training in Army boots. Worse still, I had unfortunately acquired a painful patch of raw skin on my heel.

Having survived the first twenty-four hours successfully, we felt more confident in moving about. We had learned, however, that keeping strictly to the open country, away from roads, was inhibiting our progress unduly and creating unnecessary physical difficulties for ourselves. On this second night, therefore, when we hit upon country lanes going more or less in the right direction, we made use of them and found the going much easier and certainly faster. Thanks to our little compass and cloudless, starlit skies, we were able to keep a check on our navigation.

We were, of course, alive to the greater dangers of meeting up with police or military. Cars gave us no trouble, we simply took cover when one approached, but bicycles proved a nuisance, being silent and invariably without lights. On the few occasions when we unwittingly encountered pedestrians or cyclists, we made no obvious move to avoid them in case we aroused suspicion.

* * *

That night we made good progress, and when morning came we stopped to rest in a sparsely wooded area not far from the road we had been using. Our intention was to rejoin it when darkness fell. The cover provided by the trees was not ideal but it proved good enough for us to escape the notice of the various passers-by on the road throughout the day – that was, until late afternoon. It was then that we were spotted by a couple of boys playing around on bicycles. They realized we were not locals so came over to exchange a few words and get a closer look. On discovering we were, in fact, foreigners, they were clearly intrigued and promptly peeled off, presumably to spread the news.

We thought we had better take off. But it was not yet dark, and while debating whether or not we should risk exposure, our young friends reappeared. This time they were in the company of three or four more, all with bicycles. They halted on the road opposite and just stood there staring at us.

We felt pretty uncomfortable being the centre of attraction like this and decided we had best make a move before there were any further developments. To bolt for it cross-country would only serve to confirm suspicions that we were not, as we had claimed, a couple of Germans on a walking holiday, and might set up a hue and cry. Better, we concluded, to play it cool and just set off casually along the road. Hopefully, the onlookers would lose interest.

We rejoined the road, waving farewell, optimistically, to the little assembly, and set off. But if we thought we could shake them off as easily as that, we were mistaken – they were following us wheeling their bicycles a few yards behind. They obviously sensed adventure and, like hounds on the trail, nothing was going to deter them now. They had even hatched a little plan, for suddenly two boys mounted their machines, raced past us and disappeared. Alerting the authorities ahead of us was obviously the intention. This embarrassing situation would have to be terminated quickly.

* * *

The immediately surrounding countryside was fairly open, with no visible cover – not ideal for throwing off pursuers. But a little further on, we came abreast of a field of tall cereal set back about 50yds from the road. This, we judged, would be a place to escape into and conceal ourselves.

The light had started to fade – a good sign. We braced ourselves. In a flash we turned on our heels, left the road and sprinted, half stumbling, across what proved to be a very roughly ploughed piece of ground to reach the field. It was fortunately a large one and we disappeared deep inside it before dropping down out of sight under cover of the tall, densely growing crop.

The group had been taken by surprise and reacted too late to keep in touch with us. We could hear excited voices in the distance and the barking of dogs at a nearby farm, presumably disturbed by people hunting for us. Within a quarter of an hour the disturbance had died down, and with darkness now coming to our aid, we were able to slip away safely.

But that little episode proved expensive. The following morning, when we halted for the day, Jimmy discovered that several of his precious tins of food were missing. They must have become dislodged from his belt during our dash across the ploughed field the night before.

* * *

By the third night we had reached the River Po just east of Cremona, as we had hoped. At this point it must have been about 150yds across and, it being spring, the water was high and fast-flowing. This, as we had known, was going to be a major obstacle.

We searched along the bank in the darkness for some distance vainly looking for a boat to row ourselves across in. In fact, we came on several small ones, but all were chained and locked to posts and none of them carried oars. We continued our search moving westwards, upstream towards Cremona, where there was a tall bridge spanning the river into the town.

It was slow going, as we had to circumvent numerous marshy tracts. On one occasion we wandered through a damp wooded area where we encountered the most marvellous spectacle of thousands upon thousands of fireflies sparkling silently all around us in the pitch darkness. It was an extraordinary sight and conjured up my childhood notions of fairyland.

By the time we reached the bridge, it was beginning to be light. We had feared it would be well guarded and, much to our disappointment, a closer look confirmed that indeed it was. Crossing by this means was now out of the question, so we passed under the bridge and continued along the water's edge.

* * *

Half an hour later, with the sun appearing, we found ourselves marooned on the south bank of the Po and feeling somewhat disconsolate. Early workers were already moving about, and some fishermen in boats appeared on the scene. This prompted us to conclude, reluctantly, that despite the risk, seeking their help would be our only hope of getting across.

With this in mind, we moved further along the river's edge until we came across a man sitting alone in a boat tied up against the bank some distance from the others. We approached him and, after introducing ourselves, asked him outright if he would take us across to the other side. He pointed to the Cremona bridge downstream and asked us why we didn't use it. Our somewhat transparent reply was that it was too far out of our way. We encouraged him with an offer of money, but he ignored it; instead, with something of a wry smile, he indicated to us to jump aboard. We were in luck!

We pulled away slowly from the shore and after a short while the boatman rested on his oars a second, leaned over and, winking an eye, asked, '*Inglesi?*' We quickly reassured him that we were indeed German. But he did not seem convinced and then, much to our surprise, he asked, '*Prigionieri?*' How could he have guessed so accurately? Again we laughed at such a preposterous idea.

Suddenly there was a shrill whistle and a yell from the bank which we had just left. It was clearly aimed at us, as our boatman stopped rowing and shouted something back in reply. There was an exchange of words between our boatman and the caller during which Jimmy and I quickly agreed that if our man attempted to turn back we would seize the boat. However, he resumed rowing, muttering something seemingly disparaging about 'Carabinieri'.

It was with feelings of great relief that we sprang ashore on the north bank. We were very grateful to the boatman, but our renewed offer of money was still refused. So we shook hands, waved farewell and set off. Normally at this hour we should have been hiding up, but the threat of carabinieri on the other side was a warning that we had better get clear of this area, and so we did.

It was a revelation to us to meet an Italian who, despite his shrewd guess that we were escaped enemy prisoners, was still willing to go out of his way to help us. It was clear where his sympathies lay, and we were sorry not to have been able to give him the satisfaction of knowing the truth, but we were in no position to take unnecessary risks. It made us wonder if our disappearance had been mentioned on the radio or in the press. If so, we should have to be more than ever on our toes; not everyone was likely to be as helpful as our boatman.

* * *

It was now our fourth day on the run, and although our morale was high, fatigue was slowing us down. Lack of food was having its effect, and we were spending more time than we should have searching for water to quench our persistent thirst. We were drinking it whenever and almost wherever we found it.

The next morning, we settled into a comfortable hiding place in a hedgerow on the bank of a clear stream. We consumed our meagre rations and watched as the welcome warm rays of the sun broke through. We were amused to watch a duck with a family ducklings come sailing past, although it probably meant we were closer to a farmstead than we would have wished. It was my turn to sleep and, as usual, I dozed off quickly. When I awoke, an hour later, Jimmy greeted me with, 'Look what I've got,' and produced one of the ducklings which he had caught and killed while I was sleeping. I don't think I showed quite the enthusiasm for Jimmy's enterprise that he expected. In fact, moments later, we were forced to take evasive action when a little girl, presumably from the local farm, approached, calling out while making a search along the course of the stream, obviously for the missing duckling. It was a while before we were able to crawl back and resume our rest. Children were to be avoided as much as adults. At dusk we departed, carrying the limp corpse with us in a paper bag.

* * *

Over the next three days the once distant Alps grew visibly closer as we pushed on further north. On our seventh day of freedom we reached the foothills in the region of San Pellegrino. One felt safer in the shelter of the mountains, but we were increasingly footsore and weary, quite apart from feeling the pangs of hunger.

Although we had traversed the rich food-producing heartland of Italy, it had been of no help to us. There was simply nothing to be found at this time of the year; we were too early even for the cherries. Once we came across a garden in which seed potatoes had been planted and we promptly lifted a few. No doubt, in due course, some barren patches in the potato plot would have been a source of mystery to some luckless gardener. Regrettably, these too, proved a failure. With some difficulty we managed to partly cook a couple of them in a small tin, and having eaten them in this state, the result was agonising cramps. Visions of roast duckling had long since vanished; our bird developed an odd smell and had to be discarded.

There were still some 50 miles of mountainous country to be overcome in order to reach the point on the Swiss frontier, north of Como, where we planned to cross. With increased cover from trees and bushes, and with fewer people around in these parts, we were able to travel by day as well as by night. But it was difficult terrain, and we were forced more and more to make use of roads in order to make headway. It was important that we wasted no time, as fatigue, blisters and hunger were handicaps that could only get worse the longer we took.

* * *

Very soon, we found that we could not continue walking all night without halting to sleep some of the time. But the ground was cold and the air at these higher altitudes chillier than in the plain below. Consequently, we soon woke up shivering and were forced to move on.

Our route to Como took us through the outskirts of Lecco, which, foolishly, we made no effort to bypass. It was here, around midnight, coming up to a crossroads, that we ran slap into an NCO of the Alpine Regiment, unmistakable in his pointed hat and feather. He spoke to us and, discovering we were not Italian, wanted to know who we were. We explained ourselves and I showed him my identity card, which seemed to satisfy him, although he was not too happy about Jimmy's lack of documents. However, before he got too serious, we adopted a jovial attitude, slapped him on the back, telling him how much the Germans admired the Alpini, and bade him goodnight. Fortunately, he made no fuss and we parted. Being on his own, at that time of night, he was likely to have been off duty and unarmed. In the circumstances, he probably felt it wiser not to press matters too far.

This was the first occasion on which we had been challenged since leaving camp, and we felt quite elated that we had got away with it, especially with someone in uniform. We decided that if we were stopped again we would act slightly drunk. It embarrasses people and enables one to gloss over awkward questions.

* * *

By the ninth night we were approaching Como, beyond which lay the final hurdle – the guarded frontier into Switzerland. But trudging 150 miles over difficult terrain with scarcely any food had taken a lot out of us. We were feeling pretty exhausted, both of us were limping badly with painful blisters and, I suspect, we were less mentally alert. In our eagerness to press on we were taking risks such as walking through villages instead of around them, something we would never have done earlier. Impatience was showing, just when the situation called for even greater care and control.

Abruptly, that night, on reaching the top of a ridge, we stopped in our tracks. It seemed almost unbelievable, but there, ahead of us on the distant hills, quite distinct and dotted around, were lights. Wartime Italy was blacked out; this could only be Switzerland. It was a marvellous sight and we stared, speechless. Here at last was our goal, we were in sight of freedom. What had once been only a dream had suddenly become a reality.

Those lights spurred us on, giving us a new lease of life. Our pace quickened as we pushed on along the main road leading to Como, now just a few short miles from us. The going was good, far quicker and more direct than the country lanes we had contended with for so long.

In our haste, the fact that we were slowly but surely, and for the first time, drifting into the built-up suburbs of a city, seemed almost irrelevant. Before very long we found ourselves on populated, busy roads; the dangers of our situation began to dawn on us. But by now there was little we could do about it; there was no quick exit to the safety of the countryside. We cursed ourselves for our foolishness in getting into this situation.

* * *

We strode along the pavements trying as best we could to walk normally and avoid limping. Although it was fairly late at night, there was still sufficient light for one to be seen at close range. Groups of people were moving around, but we tried to keep out of their way, avoiding, at all costs, any possible chance of contact. We hoped to strike a route that would take us into a quieter part of the city. Police would certainly be patrolling a frontier town like this at night, and a couple of young men, rather oddly dressed in civilian clothes in wartime, could arouse suspicion.

In fact, before long, we were accosted by a man in plain clothes, who stepped out of a shop doorway in front of us, announced that he was a police official and asked us who we were. We put on our pre-arranged drunk act. Jimmy was particularly good at this, taking him by the arm and trying to convince him to come with us for a drink. Meanwhile, I made sure he got a look at my German identity card with his torch, hoping it would reassure him, and then quickly put it away. He continued his attempts to question us but only drew laughter, until finally, showing some discomfort, he gave up. We shook him firmly by the hand and then staggered on our way out of sight.

It had been a very near thing and it shook us. We had never felt more sober, and the urgency of getting away from this place became more apparent. Although twice now we had been able to bluff our way out of a tight corner, in each case we were fortunate in having been confronted by a somewhat weak character acting alone.

* * *

Our hand-drawn map indicated that the most suitable crossing point into Switzerland would be some 3 miles along the wire north-west of Como. With this in mind, we kept moving northwards, hoping to clear the city and disappear into the countryside well before first light.

In due course we turned into a side street which seemed to be taking us in the right direction. It was quiet and deserted, and we were relieved to have got away from the busier main roads. Suddenly we ran into a uniformed Carabiniere officer, who immediately challenged us. He was a pompous little man and demanded to see our documents. As before, we put on the happy German act, but this time we were unlucky. He responded in fluent German – we were sunk. Naturally, he recognized immediately that he was on to something. For our part, we realized, too, that the game was up. There was no point in playing around any longer; we decided that the only thing now was to run for it.

He came after us calling on us to stop. He had a pistol in his belt, and I was wondering whether he might be tempted to use it. Instead, he started blowing a whistle. We increased our pace and were discussing separating and running in different directions at the next road junction when almost immediately we were overtaken by two soldiers of the Bersaglieri Regiment on bicycles. Presumably they were on road patrol in the vicinity and had responded to the call for help from the officer.

They dismounted, blocked our way, unslung their rifles and, pointing them at us, warned us to halt. By this time, the Carabiniere officer, somewhat breathless, had caught up with us again. We started arguing once more, but he would have none of it and convinced the soldiers that we should all proceed immediately to the nearest police station. This time there was no escape; we were marched off under escort.

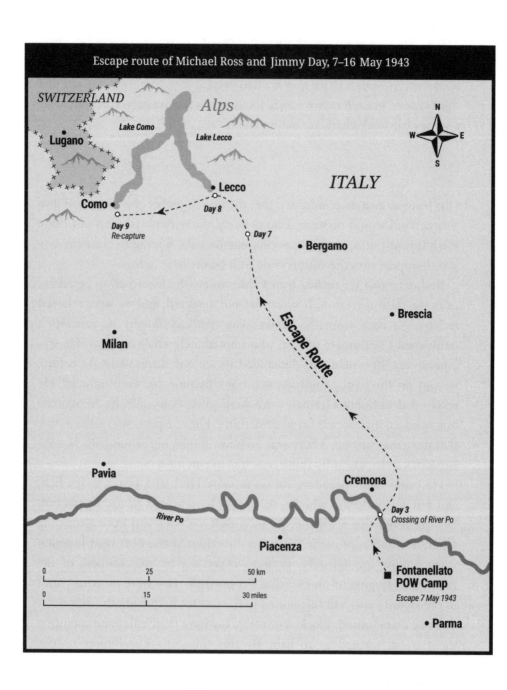

Escape route of Michael Ross and Jimmy Day, 7–16 May 1943

SWITZERLAND

Alps

Lake Como

Lake Lecco

Lugano

ITALY

Lecco

Como

Day 8

Day 9
Re-capture

Day 7

• Bergamo

• Brescia

•
Milan

•
Pavia

Cremona
•

River Po

Day 3
Crossing of River Po

Piacenza
•

■ Fontanellato
POW Camp

Escape 7 May 1943

• Parma

Escape Route

| 0 | 25 | 50 km |
| 0 | 15 | 30 miles |

Chapter 14

Enemies Become Friends

O ur little procession wound its way along a main road in silence. It was still dark, so I took the chance to dispose of my identity card discreetly before reaching the police station. I simply tore it into several pieces and dropped them on the ground as we walked along.

We did not have far to go, and when we reached our destination we were shown into a room where numerous officials descended on us and attempted to interrogate us. But we had no intention of making things easy and refused to reveal our true identity.

A senior officer then appeared and demanded to see my document. When I could not produce it, we were stripped completely, given a blanket each and told to squat on the floor. Meanwhile, a search was made of our clothing. There was, of course, no sign of the card, but then an idea occurred to the pompous carabiniere who had arrested us, and he promptly left the room armed with a big torch.

Within ten minutes he was back, face beaming, triumphantly holding up the pieces for all to see. A few nasty threats were cast in my direction as these remnants were carefully scrutinized and later placed on a table near us together with our clothes and belongings.

There followed a series of comings and goings and some heated arguments between the officials. Even the policeman in plain clothes who had let us slip through his hands earlier that evening made an appearance, looking rather sheepish. During this commotion we remained seated on the floor and at one point I was able, unnoticed, to reach up and seize the remains of my card. I hid the pieces safely inside my blanket and then asked if I could go to the toilet.

I was duly escorted to washrooms in another part of the building. Needless to say, I promptly flushed the pieces of card straight down the drain. After I returned, Jimmy and I had a quiet laugh when I whispered what I had done and suggested that our smart carabiniere would be hard pressed to retrieve the pieces this time. We also chuckled, later on, at the faces of the authorities when it dawned on them that the wretched bits of card had disappeared for a second time.

* * *

After an hour or so we were conducted to one of the cells and locked in. We wondered if they regarded us as some sort of Houdini escape experts, as they took the precaution of locking into the cell with us two hefty-looking policemen as company for the rest of the night. We sat in silence, except for one of the policemen, who whiled away the hours cracking his knuckles. In the morning we were told to dress, given a cup of black coffee, handcuffed and marched over to the main police headquarters of Como.

Here, in an upstairs room, we were once again faced with an interrogator; this one spoke good English. He started off by saying that he knew exactly who we were, and so he did. He added that our three colleagues had been caught more than a week ago. This was our first intimation that the others had, in fact, succeeded in getting out, so there was no point in our playing dumb any longer. We confirmed our personal details but said nothing more. We refused to be drawn by his enquiries as to how we had escaped and managed to reach Como. It was just possible that the camp authorities were still unaware of the means by which the five of us had got out.

* * *

We were now returned to the cells pending transportation back to Fontanellato. Meanwhile, we were given a large mess tin of meat broth and rice. It was our first hot meal in ten days and we devoured it eagerly. About midday we were taken out, handcuffed again and driven to the railway station, accompanied by three carabinieri. We boarded a Milan-bound train, where a first class compartment was unceremoniously cleared of passengers, and the five of us took our seats.

Our escorts proved to be good company which, together with the luxury of a comfortable ride on a full stomach, was something to be enjoyed. The full impact of our misfortune had not really penetrated our minds. Recapture had not been the traumatic experience one might have imagined. Having been held captive for over a year and a half, I was already adjusted to life as a prisoner. Now, I was returning to normality. A dog put back on the lead after a burst of freedom feels none the worse for it.

* * *

The senior escorting officer was holding our few belongings, which were to be handed over with us on arrival at camp. These included a few hundred lire, which we knew would be confiscated. Jimmy suggested to him that it might be appropriate to spend this money on a meal at Milan station while awaiting our connection for Piacenza. He would not hear of it at first, but by the time we had arrived, Jimmy had won him over to the idea. It was typical of Jimmy's enterprising ways.

We changed at Milan and made straight for the station restaurant. The senior carabiniere kindly agreed to the handcuffs being removed, so Jimmy and I were able to sit on stools at the bar, like any other customer, and order a cold snack. Our escorts hovered in the background, keeping an eye on us.

Somehow word must have got around quickly about who we were, for in no time the place was crowded with people eager to meet us and shake our hands. We were quite overwhelmed by the reception and could not believe the friendliness of everyone. The restaurant's chef came out to introduce himself and proudly recalled the wonderful times he had spent working at the London Savoy before the war. The smiling young waitress who served us so attentively slipped me a scrap of paper on which was written a Milan telephone number. I wondered where she thought I was going.

Having finished our meal, a way was cleared for us so we could get to the platform for the connection to Piacenza. There was almost a carnival atmosphere as people followed behind to see us off. There were farewells and waves as we boarded the train and pulled out.

We were quite breathless as we sat back in the compartment. We had certainly not anticipated this sort of reception from the local people; it was hard to believe we were at war with them. Only two days before, the news of the surrender of all Axis forces in North Africa had broken, yet the Italians we met seemed in no way depressed – in fact, just the opposite.

A truck and additional escorts were waiting for us at Piacenza station to conduct us back to Fontanellato by road. When we approached the main gates of the camp, a very different reception from the Milan experience awaited us. The Italian soldiery came running out of their quarters to meet the truck, hooting, jeering and cursing us, shaking their fists and making obscene gestures in our direction. We learned later that they had spent many fruitless nights scouring the countryside for us, so we had hardly done them a favour, and a frosty reception was to be expected.

We were immediately ushered into the commandant's office to face a rather sad-looking colonel.

'As yours was the first escape from this camp, I have decided not to send you to Garvi this time. From now on, occupy your minds with things other than escaping. Thirty days confinement. Dismiss.'

These were his final words; I felt sorry for him. He was a gentleman, and our escapade had only brought him discredit.

* * *

We were escorted back to an isolated part of the main building where we found the other three. Luckily, through lack of space, solitary confinement could not be imposed on five officers at the same time, so we were all kept together in one locked and guarded room.

We learned that the other three had got out successfully the night after us, as planned, but within hours were back in camp. Their intention had been to travel by train to Como and then cross the border into Switzerland on foot. It had the advantage of being quick and clean, although risky. Their cover story was that they were Spanish immigrant workers; Joss spoke the language fluently.

They had purchased tickets at a railway station some few hours walk from the camp and boarded a train travelling to Milan. The booking clerk, however, sensed there was something odd about three foreigners travelling up to Como and decided to alert the police. By the time they reached the next station, the police were already there waiting. The train was halted while they boarded and carried out a thorough check on passengers; the three were soon identified. After questioning them, the police were quite convinced that they were not Spanish and ordered them off the train.

The police investigations included a call to the PoW camp at Fontanellato to enquire if three prisoners were missing. The reply, at first, was, 'No, but we will check just to make sure.' They then proceeded to carry out a hundred per cent head count by name and were horrified to discover that not three but five were missing.

* * *

When nothing was heard of Jimmy and myself for nine days, it was generally assumed we had made it. Indeed, having covered some 150 miles of populated enemy territory undetected and got within sight of the frontier, it was pure stupidity and impatience that lost us the chance of completing a successful escape. Physically, it had taken a lot out of us; our faces were drawn and sunburnt, our feet were in a bad way and we had lost a great deal of weight. In the last few days, lack of food and sleep had contributed to increasing fatigue. Our craving for water had tempted us to drink indiscriminately at every opportunity. Since it was never from a tap, we were lucky not to have caught some frightful disease. Despite all this, we were soon fit again.

* * *

The other three proved to be very cheerful company, but especially entertaining was Tony Roncoroni, the England rugger player, who kept us amused with accounts of his exploits as a young man-about-town in pre-war London. The ears of many a high society lady must have been burning during those weeks we were confined together. But his speciality was murder trials. He had an uncanny memory in this field and could relate, in the greatest detail, the whole course of events of the more notorious cases. Tony had quite a repertoire of stories, and we were forever egging him on to entertain us with them. One could hardly describe confinement in such company as punishment.

But above all else, the war news that reached us was heartening. The African campaign had just ended in total victory for the Allies, and now the Eighth and First Armies would be free to strike again. It was inevitable that their next objective would be mainland Italy. Our hopes of release from prison were rising.

* * *

On completing our sentence and rejoining the others, one was immediately aware of a fresh wave of optimism throughout the camp, the more so when, in due course, Sicily was invaded and taken, to be followed soon afterwards by the Allied landings on mainland Italy.

Although still distant from the actual battle fronts, we were already witnessing signs of the approaching conflict. One afternoon we heard for the first time the unmistakable drone of large numbers of aircraft, and there was cheering in the camp when vast formations of our bombers appeared overhead at high altitude. We could even hear subsequent rumblings, somewhere to the north, indicating that targets, probably in Milan, were being attacked.

On one occasion, a plane returning from one of these missions, was seen dropping down from its formation, trailing smoke. Two white parachutes appeared while the aircraft continued to lose height rapidly and finally crashed with a loud explosion and a rising cloud of smoke not far from the camp. Our flying experts reckoned there were another five men still inside; none could have survived. Half an hour later, a military vehicle arrived at our camp bringing in one of the two crew members we had watched parachuting safely. But we were not allowed to meet him, and shortly afterwards he was driven away again. However, we did manage to send over a Red Cross parcel for him. It must have been a record for the quickest delivery ever to someone taken prisoner.

* * *

There was activity on the ground too. German troops were in evidence near the camp for the first time; certainly a bad omen for us. Occasionally, a company or so would march along the road just outside the building,

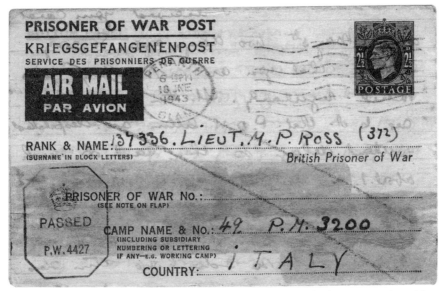

A letter to Michael from his mother on special PoW forms. The letter was redacted in parts by the MoD on security grounds. (*Ross Family Archive*)

singing Nazi hymns with much gusto, obviously for our benefit. However, most of them seemed to be passing through on their way to the newly opened front down south.

For the moment, we were confident that the German priority in Italy would be the stiffening of the Axis front in Southern Italy in the face of increasing pressure from the Allies. At the same time, the Germans would be unlikely to stand aside and watch large numbers of Allied prisoners of war held by the Italians escape to freedom in the wake of an Italian collapse.

We scoured the local papers for items of news which might indicate an early ending to Italian resistance. The first significant pointer was the fall of Mussolini and his replacement by Badoglio. The words of Badoglio's first official pronouncement on taking over – 'The war continues' – were only to be expected. But reading between the lines of some subsequent government statements quoted in the press, there were signs that the ground was being prepared for a separate Italian armistice. Even the tone of reporting was changing. One writer, for example, spoke of the traditional resolve of the British infantryman – hardly something one would have read in the old Fascist press.

The Italians seemed quite resigned to the idea that the war was lost. They did not appear unduly concerned. On the contrary, the prospect of ending the German alliance and of sweeping away the Fascist regime seemed to have considerable appeal at this time.

These developments stirred us into action as well. There was now the real possibility of being completely free of our captors in the very near future. With this in prospect, we organized ourselves into platoons, companies, etc., and officers were nominated for command and staff duties. Meanwhile, and presumably in violation of the Geneva Convention, clandestine refresher courses in military subjects became the order of the day.

* * *

Rumours of every description abounded until finally, on 8 September 1943, the Italian High Command let it be known that it had agreed an honourable end to hostilities. So the long-awaited big moment had come at last. Now the question on everyone's mind was, 'What happens to us?'

The question was soon answered by an official communication reaching the camp from Allied Headquarters.: 'Prisoners are to remain in camps and await the arrival of repatriation teams.' We were astonished at such an absurd order and concerned that our people seemed to be so completely out of touch with the realities of the situation. Kesselring had already ordered his troops to fight the Italians if need be, and judging by the gunfire we had heard the previous night, it seemed evident that some confrontations had, in fact, already taken place. It was clear to us, if not to Allied Headquarters, that there was going to be no easy exit for the likes of us from territory controlled by the Germans.

Our great fear was that, in the confusion reigning at the time, we could fall victim to orders having gone astray or being lost, enabling the Germans to descend upon the camp, take it over and carry us off to Germany.

We had recently seen for ourselves German reinforcements moving south. That could mean only one thing: with or without the Italians, the Germans intended to fight on and contest every inch of ground. If we had ever cherished hopes of an enemy tactical withdrawal to the Alps, we had no illusions now.

* * *

We were becoming apprehensive and sought urgent talks with the Italian camp commandant. He could only confirm that for the moment his orders to hold us remained unchanged. However, having said that, and entirely on his own initiative, he promised that in the event of any sign of German intervention he would set us free. That was exactly what we wanted to hear. We counted ourselves fortunate to be in the hands of a man with the courage to defy the Germans at a time like this.

Another anxious day of uncertainty passed, but at least the commandant was taking some practical precautions for our benefit. He ordered a wide gap to be cut in the perimeter wire around the field to facilitate a quick evacuation. He permitted one of our senior officers, in the company of one of his own, to leave camp and make a reconnaissance in the adjoining countryside for the purpose of selecting an area which could provide temporary concealment for us. But most important of all, he posted sentries with bicycles some distance from the camp on all roads approaching it. They had orders to return post-haste if they sighted any Germans coming our way. Meanwhile, back in camp, we practised alarm calls and emergency stations, assembling in the field in our newly organized operational formations. All we could do now was wait and hope.

* * *

We did not wait long. The following morning, just before midday, a sentry came racing back on his bicycle with news that a convoy of German vehicles was coming our way. It had been sighted drawn up on a main road about 2 miles back. The Italian commandant was true to his word and he ordered the bugler to sound the alarm. We were to be set free.

We rushed from the building and out into the field, where we formed up into our pre-arranged units. Very soon we were moving off quickly but in orderly fashion through the prepared gap in the wire fence into the open country, heading for freedom. Some Italian officers of the camp staff came with us, but the commandant stayed at his post.

Under a cloudless blue sky, our column hastily retreated from Fontanellato. We were guided along a series of country paths for several hours until we reached the wooded banks of a partly dried-up river. Here we halted and spread out under cover of the trees.

We needed a breathing space, safe from enemy search parties, to await orders, if any, from Allied HQ. So far, the only cause for concern had been a low-flying aircraft over our column earlier on. Our present whereabouts, however, were soon known to local people who appeared bearing food and wine. It was heartening to discover how very friendly the Italians were towards us. But they also brought us the sad news that when the Germans arrived at the camp and found it empty, they had arrested the commandant and carried him off. This brave man paid the penalty for his courageous stance.

* * *

By nightfall a message from our Senior British Officer was circulated ordering us to disperse that night in small groups and to endeavour to get out of German-occupied territory. The only advice was that going north and crossing into Switzerland would be safest and quickest. Attempting to penetrate the battle fronts in southern Italy to reach our own lines would be very hazardous.

Under cover of darkness, sections of ten men or so were despatched at intervals to achieve a measure of dispersal; these in turn, broke up into smaller groups of two or three. Had Jimmy Day, my former escapee colleague, been in my group, we would have gone off together once more. Prior to the evacuation, however, we had been allocated to different companies and we never met again.

In the section in which I now found myself there was only one person with whom I had more than a nodding acquaintance – it was strange how insulated one became in prison and how very narrow one's range of friendships was. He was a subaltern of the Highland Light Infantry named Cecil Bell, but generally known as George. Back in camp, we were among a small group of Roman Catholics who attended Mass together regularly on Sundays. We decided to team up.

George was a tall, fair-haired man who, pre-war, had been in tea planting in Ceylon. A somewhat stern, serious expression belied a warm-hearted nature; quiet, placid but solid, he had a ready sense of humour and was a reliable, honest character one could get along with easily. I counted myself lucky to be, quite by chance, sharing such an uncertain future in the company of a man like George.

QUESTA LAPIDE RICORDA
NEL QUARANTESIMO ANNIVERSARIO
I PRIGIONIERI DI GUERRA
INGLESI E ALLEATI
QUI INTERNATI NEL CAMPO
DI CONCENTRAMENTO P.G. 49
LA POPOLAZIONE DI
FONTANELLATO
CHE DOPO L' ARMISTIZIO
DEL 8 SETTEMBRE 1943
LI AIUTO' E LI NASCOSE
A RISCHIO DI
GRAVI RAPPRESAGLIE

FONTANELLATO 11 SETTEMBRE 1983

Plaque outside Fontanellato Camp gate commemorating the PoWs and the Italians who helped them following the Italian Armistice.

Part III

A Lame Dog

Chapter 15

On the Run to the Southern Front

It was surprising how quickly and easily several hundred of us could disappear and dissolve into the surrounding countryside. After the first day or so, it was rare to cross paths with any of the previous inmates of Fontanellato. Only at night did the frequent barking of dogs in farmsteads betray the presence of wandering strangers like ourselves.

There were, in fact, large numbers of ex-prisoners on the move, not only British but also Americans, Yugoslavs, Greeks and others. There were also Italian soldiers making for home. The threat of their units being taken over by Germans following the armistice had persuaded many to quit. All of us had sought the safety of the countryside, away from towns and main roads.

We wasted no time in getting as far away from the camp as possible and in a few days we were well into the hillier terrain of Romagna. Here we paused at a large friendly farmstead, where we were provided with food, civilian clothing and the use of a barn for sleeping. This respite gave us a chance to reflect on our situation and make plans.

The option of crossing into Switzerland we quickly dismissed. Prior to the Italian surrender, any British prisoner who managed to escape to Switzerland could expect to be spirited home through France and Spain with the help of agents. Today, the sheer number of people seeking refuge there would rule this out. The likely alternative was indefinite internment. This had no appeal to George or myself.

Sanctuary in Switzerland, though, was the only hope for marked Italian anti-Fascists who had thought the fall of Mussolini was the end of Fascism and who had publicly rejoiced at the prospect. With the Germans assuming charge of affairs and resurrecting the old regime, the diehard Fascists were back in business and anxious to avenge themselves on such people.

* * *

Back at Fontanellato, the armchair generals had forecast an early Allied landing in the Gulf of Genoa. This would have threatened to seal off the greater part of Italy at a stroke and forced the enemy northwards to a defensive line on the Alps. It seemed plausible enough, and if it materialized, then in our present location, we could hope for a timely liberation. With this in mind and encouraged by the good people of our farm, we were happy to stay put awhile and await developments.

This farm was isolated and some miles from the nearest main road, which gave added security. Nevertheless, with the political situation in turmoil and rumours of all kinds abounding, one could not afford to be complacent. One had to be particularly wary of officials and anyone in uniform. It was not easy to distinguish friend from foe.

Our warm-hearted hosts seemed indifferent to possible dangers. We had to insist on not spending nights in their home, instead retreating to the old barn. It was a comfortable place to sleep, offering concealment from surprise visitors and a quick exit in case of emergency.

Life on the farm was refreshing. The family was a large one, spanning three generations. Everyone had a task of some sort; there were no idle hands – certainly not ours. We were only too glad to offer our labour, despite the inevitable blisters. It was harvest time and the busiest season of the year.

Gradually, judging from the number of callers curious to see us, the knowledge of our presence spread to neighbouring farms. We became concerned and, despite assurances that they were all close friends and thoroughly reliable, we decided we must leave. It was the risk to the family, not ourselves, that was uppermost in our minds. We had been less than a week with them, but our departure was marked by much embracing and even tears.

We, too, were sorry to leave. One could only admire these kind, hardworking country folk, tied as they were to their farms from morning to night with no time for recreation or entertainment. Their lives were spent caring for, controlling and combating the nature around them. Helping someone in need came as naturally to them as mending a broken fence. Had the tables been turned, I think they would have readily aided a German soldier.

* * *

For the next couple of weeks we drifted southwards, sticking to open country and avoiding people as much as possible. For anyone on the run a cardinal rule was to keep moving. There was no such thing in those days as a safe place. Already stories were circulating about the misfortunes of some who thought they had found one.

We adopted the drill of waiting until evening before approaching a worker out in a field, preferably a solitary one. Engaging him in conversation usually led to an offer of food and, if we were lucky, the use of a barn or stable for the night.

We never called at an unknown house, nor did we ever approach women. They were nervous of strangers, and offers of hospitality were strictly the province of the man of the house. Exceptionally, one came across a farm where the menfolk were absent – probably on service – leaving women in charge. We met a couple of ex-prisoners who told us they had lodged for a fortnight at one such place run by two sisters. They boasted of having been made more than welcome. Such liaisons could, of course, be dangerous. Our friends wisely had second thoughts and broke them off before it was too late.

* * *

We had not lost hope of an Allied landing somewhere in the north of Italy, but as time passed, we felt the likelihood of one to be receding. From what news we were able to glean it seemed clear that large numbers of our forces were now committed in the south and, from all accounts, were under considerable pressure.

We were desperate for reliable news in the face of so many rumours. The local people, normally quite rational, were unbelievably naive in the matter of distinguishing truth from fiction. We were constantly fed with stories of how partisans had taken control of such and such an area or how ex-PoWs had been secretly evacuated from the beaches by landing craft at some place or another. We listened patiently to these tales related in all seriousness. To have shown doubt would have seemed unpatriotic, but in private we voiced scepticism.

Occasionally, we were lucky enough to hear the BBC. Happily, the official ban on listening to foreign broadcasts was everywhere ignored. There were special broadcasts to Italy, preceded by the already famous

drum beats of the 'V' sign in morse code. These often included requests
to the population to assist persons like ourselves and quite frequently
passed messages to partisans on such matters as disruption of enemy
lines of communications.

There were persistent rumours of the presence of partisans almost
everywhere we went, but we encountered no organized resistance to the
Germans. Partisans had undoubtedly been active in a number of areas;
we just happened not to find ourselves in one of them at the right time.
We should dearly have liked to make contact with them. Being entirely on
our own in strange surroundings meant that moving about and seeking
food and shelter was hazardous and imposed dangers on those helping
us. Partisans, by contrast, would know their way about, and joining them
would afford us a measure of independence.

Happily, we did on rare occasions meet up with old friends from
Fontanellato and were glad to exchange experiences and seek news.
However, just as animals in the wild do not welcome the intrusion of
rivals in their own territory, we were not overjoyed at the presence of
others, whoever they might be, if food was in the offing.

From such conversations we learned that not all camps had been as
fortunate as ours. Many, including my old camp at Padula in the south,
had been seized intact at the time of the armistice and the inmates carried
off by rail to Germany. The Padula prisoners started the journey in very
crowded open cattle trucks, and on the way up through Italy the train
halted for a moment at a country station. Among the prisoners was an
officer of my regiment called Bill Wilshire. Bill spotted a tap nearby and
promptly jumped down from the truck, ran to the tap, filled a couple of tins
with water and started back. At that moment he was seen by the German
sentry perched on the wagon. Evidently this sentry had not noticed Bill
leave the train in the first place and when he saw him approaching – Bill
was in shirt sleeves – the sentry assumed he was an Italian trying to be
helpful. Whereupon he swung his rifle at Bill and told him to clear off.
Seconds later, the train pulled out, leaving a dumbfounded Bill standing
on the platform holding a couple of tins of water – but a free man.

On another occasion we met one of our camp Dental Corps officers
who, before leaving camp, had thoughtfully armed himself with a few
simple tools of his trade. During his wanderings the word had got round
about him and he had been called upon to perform quite a number of

extractions for grateful farm folk. Doctors and dentists were rare birds in these parts. His camp dental mechanic, an RN rating, was still with him. He was now calling himself a naval lieutenant as it made things easier. He was not the first ex-prisoner on the run to promote himself for the benefit of the local population, who were invariably inquisitive about rank.

* * *

As we moved deeper and higher into the mountains, so the farms became progressively poorer. Cultivating terraces on the slopes of steep hills was arduous and often barely rewarding. Additionally, the small size of many farms, resulting from the old custom of dividing up the land between sons, meant an intense struggle to make a living out of them.

There were times when George and I withdrew tactfully from one of these poor farms, or accepted only token amounts of food, when we discovered how many young mouths were waiting to be fed from what we guessed would be very limited resources. But poverty never seemed to prevent these people from trying to help in any way they could.

The women of these farming communities were particularly hard working. Between household chores they would be out in the fields, fetching and carrying, tending to the poultry, rabbits and other animals and then going back to the house to prepare and serve meals to their returning menfolk. At the end of the day, while the men smoked or drowsed in their set places around the fire, the women would be spinning wool by hand, stripping maize or performing other seasonal tasks. It must be said, however, in fairness to the men, that a whole day spent farming the steep slopes of the upper Apennines could be exhausting. Only rarely was help available in the form of oxen for ploughing or mules for load-carrying.

There were few pleasures for these people. The men would meet occasionally at the local trattoria, while the women exchanged visits with neighbours to gossip. Sunday was observed as a day of rest, and families would congregate at the village church. It seemed customary for the women and children to enter the church to hear Mass while most of the men gathered around in groups outside to chat.

Mealtimes were the family social occasion and were taken leisurely. Table talk with us usually included a rundown on the war situation and the prospects of an early liberation of the north.

The women liked to know about our lives and families at home. Hatred of Germans was common ground; Germans were often quoted as being indifferent to the plight of Italians fighting as their allies in Russia. On the other hand, despite the grave losses inflicted on the Italian army in Africa by the British, there was no evidence of rancour towards us. Furthermore, years of anti-British propaganda by the Fascists seemed to have had surprisingly little effect. Only occasionally one detected faint echoes, as when an 8-year-old girl enlightened me on the total number of British colonies worldwide – something I had never known. She also asked me if it was true that we ate five meals a day.

Conversation was all a bit of a struggle for George and myself, with our limited Italian. I now envied those wise enough to have spent their time in captivity learning the language. But attempts by some to speak to us in English were not uncommon; they had worked in the USA pre-war and relished the chance to demonstrate their linguistic ability. Unfortunately, their efforts in fractured English were usually painful, relieved only by the odd amusing but bawdy North American expression. One almost blushed at hearing these words in mixed company. Quite clearly, their users were oblivious to their meaning.

As for the food itself, our diet was virtually vegetarian. Pasta, in its variety of forms, was the mainstay, but polenta, poured hot on to a scrubbed table top and, when firm, sliced and served, was also common fare. Tomatoes and other local vegetables would be included, and often, mushrooms. We had only ever eaten one type of mushroom, but here there was an endless selection of edible ones, picked freshly by the children in nearby woods.

Meat and dairy produce were less in evidence, being valuable commodities destined mainly for market. At times though, a small round goats' milk cheese, often alive with maggots, would appear on the table, or a lively rabbit, held by the ears might be brought in for general approval before being silenced by a single blow of the hand. Its meat would be consumed later on with pasta or rice.

Home-produced bread and wine were invariably taken with meals. These were the concern of the man of the house. After dispensing the wine, he would hold a loaf under his arm and cut thick slices in a circular movement with his clasp knife. He would then proceed to distribute them around the table on the point of the blade.

Fruit, if available, was eaten in season. Now was the time for grapes, but they were strictly consigned to the wine presses. Autumn apples were not common in our region, but there were small wild pears. Children would bake them in the oven and eat them hot. When cooked, the insides were pink and deliciously sweet. Right now, there were also blackberries in the hedgerows. George and I were only too glad to sample these but, strangely, the local people seemed to ignore them.

We were unable to repay these kind folk for the food and other help they provided. The best we could do was to leave a note with them describing what had been done for us. We always added a warning in Italian that the note should be shown only to a British or Allied officer. It was the only way to express our thanks and, hopefully, provide something of future value. Although these people were glad to accept this acknowledgement, I cannot recall a single person ever asking for it.

* * *

By now we had been at liberty for over a month. We had given up any serious belief in an Allied landing in the north and resigned ourselves to the need to push on down south. The news from the southern front was not reassuring; the hoped-for early assault on enemy positions, followed by a drive northwards, showed no sign of materializing. On the contrary, the Germans were offering stiffening resistance, and the little progress made by the Allies had been painfully slow and costly. Defensive lines were being drawn up on both sides which, combined with the onset of wintry weather, suggested a pause in operations. Under these conditions, with a stabilized front, the difficulties of breaching enemy lines unobserved and rejoining our own troops on the other side would be that much greater.

There was another option: turn back, follow the Mediterranean coastline through France into neutral Spain and exit through Gibraltar. We had heard much about the *Maquis* underground in France; they seemed well established and, doubtless, would be helpful. On balance, however, we decided it would be quicker, though riskier to keep on going south and hopefully cross the lines. We set off.

A few days later we chanced to meet a group of ex-Fontanellato inmates who had gone directly south after leaving camp but were now retracing their steps northwards. A month earlier, they had reached the combat zone and remained there for some time awaiting an opportunity of getting through the lines. After witnessing the misfortunes of many colleagues who had tried, they concluded the risks were too great and decided to turn back. Meeting up with this group and listening to their experiences finally convinced us. We changed our minds; we were going to France.

Chapter 16

Change of Plan – Westwards through France

It was well into the autumn of 1943 when we turned round and headed north-west. Our intention was to keep to the mountains and follow them, parallel to the coast, through Liguria and into France.

The weather was turning cold, and whilst lack of warm clothes was no problem, travelling on foot by day and passing the night under hedgerows was starting to lose its appeal.

Farmhouses with barns or stables were now our objective at the end of each day. Stables, in particular, were ideal. Not only did they have a bay at one end filled with straw where we could sleep, but the whole place was kept beautifully warm all night by the steaming bodies of the cattle – a most efficient central heating system.

There were usually a few pigs sharing the stables as well, but they were not our favourite companions, being both noisy and smelly. And then there was the occasion when one of them almost relieved me of my boots. I had taken them off as usual before lying down for the night. In the morning I woke up to discover a hungry pig happily munching away at them. Fortunately, I was in time to effect a rescue. Losing one's boots in our situation could have been disastrous.

The cows, by comparison, were quiet, well-behaved beasts, their only diversion being an occasional release of dung or splash of urine on the stony floors. The strength of ammonia from the latter could really burn the eyes.

Completing the company were the poultry, who normally perched above the straw bay. They did not adjust easily to intruders like ourselves lying below them and could take a long time to settle down to their customary roosting plan. But at dawn there was a general exodus and they all cleared out to join the dawn chorus long before we were ready to leave.

Once, when occupying a barn, we could not get to sleep because of the incessant miaowing of a cat prowling around outside. We felt so frustrated that George decided to smoke one of his precious cigarettes, before the fire risk suddenly dawned on him and he put it out. We joked about having to add a postscript to our usual note of thanks in the morning regretting that we had burned down the good farmer's barn. But the cat did not give up, and at daylight, when we sat up to remove the straw from our hair and clothes, we discovered the reason for her anguish. Unwittingly, we had been lying all night alongside a nest of her kittens hidden in the straw.

* * *

Each morning, before setting off, we made a point of scanning the horizon and choosing some well-defined feature as a direction indicator for our line of march. On one such occasion we sighted a distant church spire on our intended route and so set off towards it. It was high up, and we reached it by mid-afternoon.

The chapel stood alone, but attached to one side of it was a small two-storey house, probably a presbytery. There were no other houses in the immediate vicinity. While we were watching the place, a woman called at the house. The door was opened by a priest, to whom she handed a basket and then took her leave. Having eaten nothing that day, we decided it was worth breaking our rule and calling at the house ourselves. The clergy were known to be trustworthy and charitable.

The door was opened, as before, by the priest. When we explained who we were, we were immediately invited inside. He was young, jovial, well fed and clearly delighted to have our company – it seemed he lived on his own. He was quick to grasp our material needs and promptly motioned us to chairs at his table. He then produced plates of cold chicken, hard-boiled eggs, cheese, bread and sweet, dark grapes. It was our best meal since leaving camp. But his hospitality did not end there. He explained that there was an empty guest room upstairs and suggested we stay on for a while to rest.

Naturally, we were delighted with the prospect and gladly accepted. Thinking about security, we were satisfied that no one had seen us enter the house, while the priest assured us that no German had ever been seen in these remote parts.

Our room upstairs had a four-poster double bed with the thickest eiderdown I had ever seen. But what intrigued us was a square cavity in the wall, into which one could put one's head, peer down a narrow shaft and get a bird's-eye view of the altar in the adjacent chapel below. We were curious about this, and our host explained that, according to legend, a parish priest had once secretly given refuge to a young unmarried woman who was pregnant. Not wishing any of this to be known, he had hidden her in the bedroom for many months. The hole in the wall had been made to enable her to hear Mass every Sunday unobserved, and so fulfil her religious duties.

After three days in the house we thought it time to move on. In any case, the stock of food was showing signs of drying up – not surprisingly, with two extra mouths to feed. Its supply in any case was unpredictable as it depended on the day-to-day charity of the pastor's flock.

At dawn next morning we ventured out into the church and attended the priest's early Mass. The congregation consisted of three elderly women all in the usual black dresses and headscarves. There was no altar boy to serve at Mass so I assisted instead – the ritual and Latin responses were identical to those practised by me years before as an altar boy in my home parish. Mass was followed by a quick breakfast of grapes and bread. We really felt much better for the comfortable rest and regular food we had enjoyed. Having thanked the good priest for all his kindness and received his parting blessing, we took our leave.

* * *

We made steady progress for the next few days, but then the onset of heavy autumnal rains forced us to seek frequent shelter. Wet clothes, and particularly wet boots, were a great discomfort, and the lack of any means to dry them out meant enduring it for long periods. In fact, clothes were becoming a problem. To avoid recognition, we had, early on, gladly exchanged our khaki battle dress for civilian trousers and jackets. Now we recognized only too well the value in our circumstances of hard-wearing military uniform. Our present garments were not designed to withstand this sort of usage and became easily torn and ragged. Some old colleagues whom we ran into had purposely not discarded their uniforms. They reminded us, cheerfully, that a soldier caught in civilian dress behind enemy lines could legitimately be shot as a spy.

One evening while moving westwards through the more remote regions of the Apennines, some 50 miles inland from Genoa, we came to two villages which, according to our map, were Bardi and Varsi. Now these two names were familiar to us.

In the early days of our freedom, stories had circulated about the very generous hospitality shown to Allied ex-prisoners by the inhabitants of these two particular places. Apparently, many of the townsfolk had, before the war, made fortunes in Britain and America and returned to settle here. They were reputed to have handed out much food, clothing and even money.

We approached a man working alone in a nearby field to enquire about the present situation in these villages. He seemed offhand and unfriendly. He was quick to warn us that some people in these parts had been punished for assisting Allied soldiers and that no one was helping them any longer.

To be greeted by this sort of remark usually meant that the person concerned was nervous about getting involved. Whenever we sensed this we wasted no time in moving on. So I mumbled to George, 'I think he's a bit windy, let's go.'

We waved him farewell and were walking away when, suddenly, he called out after us in the most pronounced Welsh accent, 'Yes, I'm windy all right!' He had understood us perfectly.

Naturally, we were taken aback by this sudden unexpected outburst, and he explained that he had lived in Wales for many years. His earlier caution, he admitted, was because of his fear that we might have been Germans posing as British to catch out would-be sympathetic locals. It was not unknown for this to have been done. Now that he was reassured, he pointed to an isolated farmhouse and invited us to call there after dark.

That night, we met him again and had supper together. He told us that before the war he had worked in Port Talbot steelworks in South Wales. Having spent much of my youth in nearby Penarth, we were able to share reminiscences of the old days. After supper we retired to his barn for the night, and before leaving next morning, his children brought us breakfast – hot milk and bread.

* * *

The relief and euphoria which had greeted the fall of Mussolini together with Badoglio's declaration of an end to hostilities had long evaporated. The Germans had wasted no time in recruiting new Italian army units named *Brigate Nere* (Black Brigades) to replace those which had melted away after the armistice. Call-up notices for men of military age were posted around regularly. The grim realities of war were returning, and there was no escaping them now.

The Allied bombing of northern Italian cities had not ceased with the armistice and were a matter of much bewilderment to some people. Occasionally we met refugees from these places who had fled to their cousins in the country to escape the danger. It was embarrassing for us to listen to their tales of the casualties and chaos caused by these attacks.

We were conscious of a growing fear amongst the population of the reprisals threatened by the authorities against anyone found helping people like ourselves. Partisans were warned by the Germans that any act of sabotage would be punishable by death. Accounts of the harassment of the enemy by members of the resistance, once common, were heard less frequently these days. Instead, most of the stories circulating were concerned with German atrocities against Italian civilians. These stories we took seriously and, sadly, it was not long before we met the reality, in this instance the aftermath of a tragic local event.

* * *

It happened in the vicinity of Monte Maggiorasca. It was a clear bright morning, and after a long climb up same rough high ground we came to an ancient farmhouse. As it was near midday, we entertained the usual hope of being stopped by the occupants and offered something to eat. A group of children were sitting on the wall of the yard as we made our approach, but when we drew nearer and saw how very poorly they were dressed we decided to keep going. Our presence, strangely, had brought no reaction from them; they were oddly quiet. Just then two women emerged from the house, both obviously in a state of some distress. We wondered what was the matter and asked them if there was anything we could do. It was then that we learned that the father of these children had been arrested the day before. He had been taken down to the town in the valley below with some others, forced into an empty garage and shot. The place had then been set on fire.

These woman were now trying to care for the afflicted family, all of whom were clearly overcome by the disaster which had befallen them. We found it difficult to understand all they were trying to say and we never discovered the reason for what had happened. The blank faces of those children I shall never forget.

* * *

Fortunately, there were also happier moments. Some days later, when passing through a large vineyard, we met a group of five or six young workers. They were on the point of retiring for their midday meal and insisted on our joining them. It was comforting to come across people who made one feel totally welcome and who were genuinely without qualms about being with us.

We all went off together to their farmstead and down into a cellar. Inside was a row of large vats containing, they said, newly laid down wine. We sat around on benches as generous quantities of the rich red liquid were drawn from the vats and passed round. The wine had not yet matured; it was sweet and bubbly and tasted delicious. Everyone was in high spirits, and laughter came easily as more wine was drawn and glasses refilled.

Before long, their womenfolk appeared with food, which was an occasion for more banter and jollity. They brought dishes of sliced yellow polenta filled with tomato and cheese. Even with two extra guests there was more than enough, so we ate our fill, enjoying it immensely.

More wine was circulated and it was well into the afternoon before the party finally broke up. George and I reluctantly dragged ourselves away.

We were given a big send-off as we waved goodbye and stepped out on to the trail once more.

* * *

Following the backbone of the Apennines, north of Genoa, we passed within sight of the town of Garvi. Figuring prominently on the skyline was the famous huge fortress which had been used as a special security prison for all Allied officers who had ever attempted to escape from camps in Italy. But for a forgiving commandant, I should certainly have been transferred here as a punishment following my escape last May from Fontanellato. I could now count my blessings, for we learned that at the time of the armistice the inmates of Garvi were handed over to the Germans to be carried off to the Fatherland. The place was now deserted.

* * *

We reached the province of Piedmont by the beginning of November and entered a region of vast sweet chestnut forests. The annual fall of chestnuts was being gathered and the process of dehydrating them over slow-burning fires was now under way. The hard white kernel formed the basis of the local economy from which the peasants struggled to eke out a living. The bulk of the produce was marketed, but the community also depended upon it as an important source of food for their own consumption. They milled the dry chestnut into powder form and used it as flour substitute for making bread and pasta. It was also the main ingredient of a traditional cake, popular throughout Italy, called *castagnaccio*.

We walked through this wooded country for several days; it was hard work and slow going. Eventually, one evening, we emerged at the head of a long, deep valley overlooking the large market town of Bagnasco.

Just then we crossed paths with a couple of youths and exchanged a few words. Apparently they were on their way home after a day's toil on the land. On learning who we were, they invited us to accompany them to their home for a meal. We pointed out that we were in no fit state to enter anyone's home as we were soaking wet, having just extricated ourselves from all sorts of trouble attempting to ford a fast-flowing torrent. But they insisted, so we went along.

On arrival we were introduced to the family, which included seven grown-up sons and one young teenage daughter. They could not do enough for us. A hot bath and a loan of clothes while our own were dried out and repaired was followed by a hearty supper. Sleeping in their barn was out of the question – we were to occupy a proper bedroom for the night. Nor did their concern for our welfare end there. Between them they thought up a plan to help us along our way on the morrow. It was suggested that we take a train from the local station in Bagnasco to a place called Ormea, a small town at the end of the line some 25km distant. It lay exactly in the direction we intended travelling and, they argued, this would save us at least a day's hard foot-slogging over difficult country.

It was tempting, but we explained that we never used public transport – we had no money anyway – as the risk of being picked up was not worth it. Our rule was to avoid all well-populated places. They pointed out that there were no identity checks or even barriers to pass through, as the station was the open type; neither need we worry about contact with officials, as the rail tickets would be bought for us. Furthermore, we would not be conspicuous, as these trains were invariably crowded with local people going to and from market.

They were full of enthusiasm, and whilst naturally we were more than grateful for everything they had already done for us, we were quietly just a little apprehensive about any plans which involved mixing with crowds for the first time. We did not, of course, show this, and all was agreed. We thanked them most profusely for all their help and then retired for the night to the comfort of a real bed.

After breakfast, two of the brothers set off for the station, while we trailed some distance behind. On arrival, we joined the throng of passengers already waiting on the crowded platform. Meanwhile, the brothers obtained rail tickets, came over close to where we were standing and waited.

The train came in and the crowd surged forward. At that moment, tickets were thrust unobtrusively into our hands. George and I immediately boarded the train at different ends of the same carriage. It seemed heartless to take our leave of such kind and brave people without a parting word or handshake. We joined those in the packed gangway, intentionally keeping some distance from each other but within sight. The train pulled out and we were on our way.

It was a wonderful, dream-like sensation watching the countryside flying past so effortlessly and at such speed; it almost felt like cheating. But I was soon jolted back to reality by the appearance of a uniformed inspector making his way through the coach, examining tickets. I felt trapped as he approached me. He took my ticket and without uttering a word or even looking up, punched it and moved on. I watched as it came to George's turn. George was wearing an old hat which concealed his blond hair but he was still conspicuous by his height, being head and shoulders above those around him. Again the inspector did not glance up; he simply checked his ticket and passed on. As he disappeared into the next coach, George and I casually exchanged looks. We could relax.

On arrival at Ormea, we left the train independently and, when clear of the station and people, joined forces again, chuckling at our good fortune. We were heartened by the success of this unexpected bonus of a smooth, fast ride over so many miles of rugged country.

A few days later, we had reason to feel less pleased when we were hit by a new, and for us serious, hazard – snow. Having to contend with this without adequate clothing meant slow progress and constantly wet feet. But unwelcome as it was in our situation, one could not at the same time fail to marvel at the spectacle of the countryside under winter's first fresh fall of snow, especially the colourful splendour of mountain peaks at dusk. The snow brought about complete stillness and total silence, as if the whole of nature had been muted.

* * *

Up to this point we had been heading due west towards the French frontier, now in sight some 20 miles away. But faced with this latest hazard, we decided to descend to the lower, less formidable reaches of the Apennines nearer the coast, where we would be below the snowline. From there we could then redirect our steps westward once more by following the coast along the Riviera. These parts would, of course, be more populated, but with luck, two or three days should see us over the frontier.

George and I discussed the prospect of venturing into a new country and wondered if we would find the same sympathy among French people. We reminisced about our two months spent on the run in Italy, the spontaneous generosity of the country folk and their unfailing courage in helping us regardless of the risks. We had come to cherish the natural warmth of these people and to admire their industry. Life in these high-altitude farming communities was incredibly hard. It was a constant struggle to extract a living from the narrow terraces of precious soil which clung to mountain slopes with the help of ancient contour-like stone walls. Manpower was short, the occasional help coming only from lethargic oxen or stubborn mules. The younger generation, if not drafted into the forces, were drifting into the towns, forsaking a way of life that had not changed in a thousand years.

It was close to the end of an era, and these folk knew they were being left behind. For them the future was only bleak and negative. I felt sad for them and sad to be leaving them but took comfort in the thought that no harm had, to our knowledge, ever come to them because of us. To have shared even such a brief part of their way of life had been a privilege.

* * *

To reach the lower regions we circumvented two prominent landmarks, Monte Monega and Monte Ceppo. Both were high mountains with no visible signs of habitation other than the odd isolated stone barracks in well-elevated positions. These formed part of a chain of army posts sited behind the frontier. The ones we spotted were manned, so we gave them a wide birth as they were likely to be sending out patrols.

Another day, and having dropped down to some 3,000ft to within 10 miles of the coast, we came across one of those typically picturesque

Italian mountain villages perched high up at the end of a ridge. It was here on a late wintry afternoon in the fading light, among some chestnut woods above the village, that we stumbled across Renato Brunati. That meeting was to change the entire course of events for us.

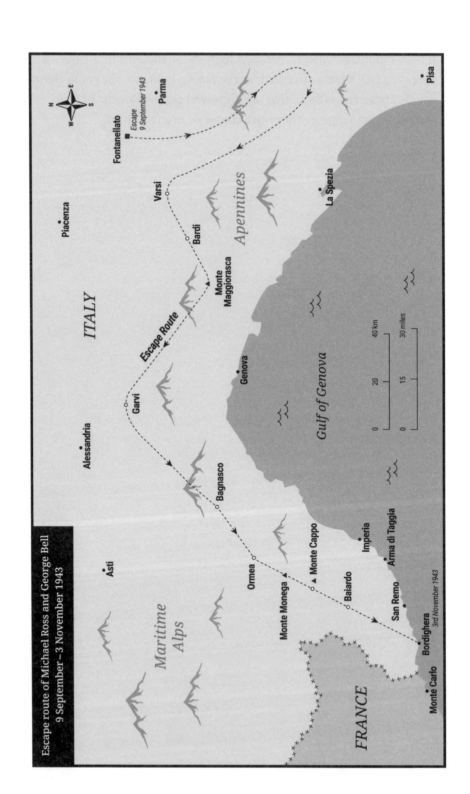

Escape route of Michael Ross and George Bell
9 September – 3 November 1943

Chapter 17

Chance Meeting with the 'Resistance'

W e exchanged greetings and asked him the name of the village. 'Baiardo', he replied, in a sullen and offhand manner. We then made the usual enquiries about the local situation and told him who we were. Once convinced that we were indeed English – most foreigners around at these times were German – his manner completely changed and he invited us to accompany him. He led us through the woods to a large villa just outside Baiardo, and the reason for his initial apprehension was soon clear.

Brunati turned out to be the leading light of a band of seven or eight anti-Fascists, aged between twenty and thirty, who were taking refuge in this villa. The owner was Lina Meiffret, the only woman in the company. Most of them were from San Remo, a large town on the coast about 10 miles away, and had forsaken their homes to avoid possible arrest for offences such as indulging in anti-Fascist activities or refusing to comply with call-up orders.

Brunati was tall, swarthy and ungainly, with black curly hair, soft brown eyes and large teeth. He was a generous, warm-hearted man, an intellectual with a love of literature and poetry. In his present political role he jokingly likened himself to Byron. He would voice, with feeling and enthusiasm, his left wing views, in which he was well supported by Lina, his friend and companion. They were both idealists and dreamers, somewhat remote, it seemed to me, from the practicalities of life.

Lina was calm and phlegmatic, gentle by nature but with a strong core of determination. She was slow but sure in speech, with a good command of English. Her appearance was her least concern; she normally wore a woollen cloche hat pulled over her ears from which hung long, straight, fair hair resting on her shoulders. Her large, limpid eyes looked out sadly above a prominent nose and mouth. She and Brunati were typical of the free-thinking liberals who courageously refused to conform to the Fascist way of life. Lina was usually followed around by a large, black, unruly mongrel belonging to Brunati which completed the trio.

George and I were made very welcome at the villa. For us it was refreshing and reassuring to be, at long last, among people openly opposed to the Germans. Up until then we had only known those who, whilst sympathetic and helpful, were just leading their normal lives and, understandably, were disturbed by our presence. But not this group.

At first they naively believed us to be Special Service officers sent into the area to make contact with people like themselves. We quickly dispelled this notion, but our presence, I liked to think, nevertheless provided some inspiration and encouragement at that time. As for operating as partisans, they had only one rifle between them, so were hardly equipped for the role.

At the time of our arrival we felt pretty exhausted, having spent many nights without proper shelter during a spell of foul weather. Now, with the comfort and warmth of a real bed, we slept the clock round. We awoke the next day to the glare from a fresh fall of snow and learned later that our behaviour had prompted one of their number to remark that if the British on the front down south were as lively as these two, it would be a long while before the north was liberated.

* * *

While Baiardo offered a welcome temporary home, we were keen to keep on the move. In particular, we were anxious to cross over the mountain barrier into France, which was now finally within reach. But our friends discouraged us from attempting it without a guide because, they claimed, the border was well manned and with the onset of snow the going could be hazardous. Better, they said, to wait here a while.

We stressed to them the importance of absolute secrecy with regard to our being there. Whilst their own presence would arouse no particular interest locally, the arrival of two British officers would be a very different matter. If the news got out it would spread rapidly, with dangerous consequences for everyone.

Baiardo itself was relatively safe. It stood at the top end of a winding road stretching 10 miles from the coast and, so far, was clear of Germans.

Nevertheless, a change of location, it was agreed, would do us no harm. So it was decided that we should all move out into the country to a remote hut, a mile distant, owned by one of the group. It could sleep eight and was reasonably well hidden. From there we would have ample warning if the enemy ever appeared at Baiardo village.

* * *

We left after dark on our third day at the villa carrying essential supplies for a short stay. Our route followed some muddy and stony trails and frequently took us through thick undergrowth. At one stage Brunati's lusty dog must have scented a rat for he suddenly tugged violently on his lead, catching Brunati off balance and dragging him headlong into a prickly bush. Our rule of silence on night marches was compromised by some muted curses, but we reached our destination within the hour without further incident.

The hut was one of those typical stone structures to be found everywhere in the Italian countryside. They were used to store agricultural implements or produce, and sometimes animal fodder.

Ours was on a steep slope close to a well. It consisted of a single room with a cave-like cellar underneath suitable for use as a kitchen. The roof seemed sound, so it would be dry even if cold. Four bunk beds had been fitted inside, complete with straw. Each was large enough to sleep two.

On the first morning Brunati complained of an uncomfortable night. This was unusual, as physical discomfort normally mattered little to him. He was also puzzled by the disappearance of his precious rifle. All was explained when the weapon was found under the straw on his bunk.

The days passed peacefully; George and I spending much of the time searching for wood for cooking and heating. We were careful to keep well clear of any locals who passed through the area. Meanwhile, Lina and Brunati had gone off to investigate the possibility of finding a guide to take us over the frontier.

* * *

On their return, they brought news that it had not been possible to find a guide for France but that they had met a fisherman who said he would be willing to take us by boat to Corsica – this island had recently fallen into Allied hands. It was heartening news and a far better alternative in any case. It would involve a sea crossing of just under 100 miles, and if successful would bring us immediate freedom.

Whilst down on the coast, Lina and Brunati had also made a point of consulting the head of the local Committee of Liberation. These committees had been set up secretly by anti-Fascists in German-occupied Italy with the object of helping resistance groups and coordinating underground activities. The local head was Giuseppe (Beppe) Porcheddu, a close friend of theirs who lived at Arziglia, next to the sea resort of Bordighera. He had suggested that the two Englishmen move down to his place and lie low, while Lina and Brunati completed arrangements with the fisherman.

* * *

The next evening, the four of us set off and, after a night's tramping over deserted mountain tracks, reached the coast at Arziglia.

It was already light as we emerged from a wooded slope to join the main road. George and I waited while Lina and Brunati went ahead. A little way along the road they disappeared into a garden through a pair of tall iron gates. The road remained quiet, so we followed on quickly. Inside the garden a short pebbled drive through a grove of palm and fir trees led to an imposing white-walled villa. The name 'Llo di Mare' had been inscribed on the front gate – this was the home of Beppe Porcheddu. We were soon ushered into the house, where we were greeted by the whole family. There was Beppe himself, his wife Rita, their 18-year-old twin daughters, Giovanna and Ninilla, and a younger son, Bitita.

We had already heard much about Beppe. He was the son of one of Italy's most renowned engineers and architects. Beppe had achieved fame in his own right as an artist and illustrator, and like his father before him, had been knighted for his achievements. As an officer in the First World War he had sustained a serious leg wound and could now walk only with the aid of a stick. Like many intellectuals of his age he had suffered in later life for his outspoken criticism of Fascism. It was evidence of the courage of the man that he should be involving himself in a cause that was becoming increasingly dangerous to serve.

* * *

Lina and Brunati went off straight away to contact the fisherman and make arrangements for our escape. Meanwhile, we remained at the villa. It was a novel experience and refreshing for us to share the company of what proved to be such a happy, intelligent family and to enjoy the luxuries and amenities of such a comfortable home. Throughout the day we listened eagerly to news broadcasts from Radio London – a great bonus – and in the evenings were entertained by the very accomplished piano playing of the twins, with Bitita on the violin. In different circumstances it could have been blissful, but the ever present cloud of uncertainty and danger, although never referred to, inevitably overshadowed everything.

* * *

After three days Lina and Brunati returned to Llo di Mare, but the news they brought was disappointing. The fisherman had gone away and his whereabouts were unknown. That night, after dark, the four of us set off once more for Baiardo.

The situation up there was unchanged, except that a couple of new faces were in evidence among the group in the hut. This did not please us, as we could never be sure that newcomers might not be tempted to boast to friends of having met with British officers. For our part we were invariably silent about our movements past and planned, especially with strangers.

Another week went by with still no news of a guide for the frontier, so Brunati suggested a change of location. He owned a villa on the coast near Bordighera which he used from time to time, and as it had been empty for several weeks he felt it would be safe to move in for a while. It was close to Llo di Mare, so he could call on Beppe again to consult him. Once more the four of us left Baiardo and trekked over the mountains to the coast.

* * *

We reached the villa early in the morning. It lay on a steep slope facing the sea, with the railway below and the main road above. Shortly after our arrival the caretaker of the villa next door, a trusted friend called Luigi, turned up with provisions. He kept an eye on things for Brunati and reported that all had been quiet recently. Fortunately, there was another trusted friend in the locality, Dr Angelo Giribaldi. He was called in to attend to Lina, who was nursing a very painful dislocated shoulder following a nasty fall the night before on our way down.

The place was somewhat bleak and chilly, but spacious and a welcome change from the overcrowded hut. A plaque on one of the walls claimed that the author Giovanni Ruffini had written his novel *Doctor Antonio* while staying at the villa. The book had inspired great interest in these parts and, it is said, contributed largely to the influx of British expatriates and the creation of the famous 'English Colony' in Bordighera at the turn of the century, at which time they outnumbered the local people. Most had long since gone, but they founded the town's only library, museum and tennis club and left behind an Anglican church and many prominent villas and tropical gardens, as well as a permanent British cemetery.

* * *

George and I made a point of always reconnoitring any new place with a view to a quick getaway in case of emergency. We were also careful to keep our few belongings together in an accessible spot to ensure no evidence of our presence was ever left behind. In this house it was more than ever essential to be on our guard as it was uncomfortably close to a main road. Brunati's past antipathy towards some important local Fascists had left him a marked man. Patrolling police, therefore, could be expected to make the odd call at his villa just to see what was going on. For him to be caught in our company would indeed be serious.

On that first morning we had an early breakfast of black coffee and rolls, after which Lina lay down to rest her battered shoulder while George and I browsed through some English books and Brunati pottered around the kitchen preparing a meal.

Just before midday there was a call from Brunati to join him for lunch. We were making our way towards the kitchen when suddenly we were startled by a loud rapping on the main door. In a flash we were back in our bedroom; we seized our belongings and waited. Lina burst in, wide-eyed and anxious.

'Carabinieri,' she whispered.

The door had not yet been opened to the callers, so George and I were able to slip out quietly into the hall and along the passageway to a bathroom at the rear of the house. From here we could look down on the back garden; there was no one there. We climbed through the window, dropped down into the garden and descended a steep, wooded slope until we reached the railway. A short distance on, we disappeared into the mouth of a tunnel. We went deep inside where it was completely dark and remained hidden. We encountered no one.

* * *

At nightfall we emerged and climbed the slope back to the house. There were no lights anywhere and all the shutters had been closed. The place was deserted. Up on the road there were no signs of any cars, so we decided to call on Luigi next door to find out what had happened.

Luigi got something of a fright when we appeared. He beckoned us in quickly and shut the door behind us. He explained that both Lina and Brunati had been taken away. Brunati had deposited his keys with him before leaving and had mentioned that they were wanted for questioning in connection with the distribution of subversive literature. Beppe, over at Llo di Mare, had already been informed of the arrests, so Luigi decided to go over again to tell him that we were safe.

An hour later, he was back with instructions to escort us over to Beppe's place. Leading the way over some tortuous hilly paths and agricultural terraces in order to avoid the main road, Luigi brought us to Llo di Mare. On arrival we found three youths waiting in the garden with bicycles. We had met them briefly during our previous stay at the villa. They were Vincenzo Gismondi, Federico Assandria and Elio Muraglio, whose families were all trusted friends of the Porcheddus.

* * *

Beppe had summoned them to conduct us to a disused house near the tiny village of Negi, high up at the top end of a valley several miles from the coast. With the arrest of Lina and Brunati there was the danger that other anti-Fascist friends, including Beppe, might also be rounded up. It was obviously unwise for us, and even for these young men, to remain in the area.

With a supply of food and blankets, the five of us set off that night on bicycles, George and I riding on the crossbars. Half way up the valley, the road came to an end at a village called Vallebona, so we concealed the bicycles and continued on foot. After several hours' walking we finally reached Negi about midnight.

Negi consisted of a scattered group of old stone houses. Ours was in a cluster of small buildings, separated by narrow, cobbled passages and arches. The place was uninhabited. We occupied a top floor room with clear views of the valley below. It had a stove for cooking as well as a table and bench. A room elsewhere with bunks provided sleeping quarters. Negi was well elevated with plenty of wooded cover around – it was also beyond the reach of vehicles – so altogether it made an ideal hideout.

The three youths proved to be cheerful company; they were high-spirited, and we all got along happily together. Elio, in particular, who had served in the Italian Airforce, had a fund of amusing stories, usually at the expense of the Germans. Vincenzo was from a well known local family. One of his ancestors had been British Vice-Consul at nearby San Remo during the British siege of Toulon in 1793 and had been in contact with Admiral Hood, commander of the Mediterranean Fleet. Vincenzo was also destined for the navy but, like Elio, had quit the service at the time of the armistice, not wishing to serve under the Germans. They were both now lying low to avoid recall. Federico had been just too young for military service, but was keeping a low profile nonetheless.

Vincenzo and Federico raised with us the feasibility, if a boat could be found, of the four of us crossing over to Corsica. Naturally, we were all for it but pointed out that it was not going to be all that easy. Firstly, enemy sea patrols from the port of Savona were operating in these waters and army units were deployed along the coast keeping it under constant surveillance. Secondly, a small rowing boat would be very vulnerable in the kind of bad weather that could blow up suddenly in these parts in midwinter. Anyway, we were the last to be discouraging; we were fortunate to have colleagues like these, prepared to take the risks. Also, they could search around for a boat and equipment discreetly without arousing suspicion, something we certainly could not do.

We spent two weeks at Negi, during which time the boys came and went. Food was a bit of a problem. It was obtained wherever and whenever, normally on the black market. On one happy occasion Beppe's family arrived en masse, bringing food and wine. We were able to enjoy a splendid meal cooked, gallantly, by Rita on our primitive wood-burning stove. Another time, Federico's sister turned up with food for him. On this occasion, George and I kept out of the way. She had not been told about us, so was best left in ignorance.

Progress was being made on the Corsica project. Vincenzo, with help from the resistance group in Genoa, had already acquired a small outboard engine and brought it back to Bordighera in a rucksack. A suitable boat, however, was proving difficult to find, especially as the authorities had ordered all privately owned boats removed from beaches. Then there was fuel, oars and other equipment, all of which was taking time to assemble. In the circumstances, it was considered better for the boys to remain in Bordighera and for George and I to move on and rejoin the group still in Baiardo to await developments.

* * *

Within a week, the boys came up to Baiardo with the heartening news that all was ready. A boat had been discovered locked up in a boathouse at the bottom of the garden of a villa by the sea near Arziglia. It would be a simple matter to break into the boathouse, lift the craft out and carry it the 20yds or so across the beach to the water's edge. All the necessary stores had been obtained and hidden in a dump just above this villa. Vincenzo had even made a special plate to clamp on to the stern of the boat and hold the outboard motor. We were lucky to have such enterprising accomplices.

Our plan was to seize the boat under cover of darkness, row out for a couple of hours, taking us beyond earshot of land, then start up the engine and get under way. Enemy patrols were infrequent, so with ten hours of darkness and hopefully blessed with good weather, there was every prospect of getting within reach of Corsica.

* * *

We left Baiardo once again, descending the steep slopes of Monte Caggio en route as we had done many times before, passed through Negi and by next evening were back on the coast. As soon as it was dark we collected the stores from where they were hidden, carried them across the road, down through the garden of the villa and dropped them alongside the boathouse. There was a window on one side, and peering through it, I could just make out the shape of an open boat about 12ft long. It was an exciting moment.

Silently, we broke the lock on the doors, opened them wide and lifted the boat out and across the stony beach into the water. Three extra men had come from Baiardo to help, which was fortunate, as the boat proved very heavy. We then fetched the stores, which included two pair of oars, and put them aboard.

Vincenzo climbed in first and sat at the prow to fix the rowlocks and oars ready for pulling away. The rest of us pushed on the stern until the craft was free of the beach. In subdued voices we bade farewell to our colleagues, who disappeared into the darkness. George, Federico and I scrambled aboard.

We had rowed out for some 50yds when we discovered, to our dismay, that water was creeping over our boots. Bailing out proved futile. It was quite impossible to stem the ever increasing flow of water through the sides of the vessel. The overlapping boards of the hull had evidently shrunk and opened up through being out of the water too long. There was nothing we could do but turn about and head back.

The boat sank ever deeper in the water and became increasingly difficult to manoeuvre. There was, however, a gentle sea swell which helped us to drift in slowly until we grounded firmly among the breakers. The boat was now completely waterlogged. We set about salvaging the equipment, but the boat itself simply could not be moved and we had to abandon it.

We beat a hasty retreat from the beach and scrambled through the garden and back up to the main road. Vincenzo and Federico hurried off to their respective homes in Bordighera, while George and I made tracks to the nearby sanctuary of Llo di Mare and the Porcheddu family.

* * *

We arrived at the doorstep dripping wet but, as usual, were welcomed without hesitation. Beppe suggested we remain there for the time being. No one could know of our presence other than our trusted friends Vincenzo and Federico. In any case, things were rather quiet just then as it was the week of Christmas.

By the next day the abandoned boat must have been discovered, but there were no repercussions as far as we knew. We concluded it must have been considered a straightforward case of theft and ended there.

We spent the festive season with the family and, despite the troubles, Rita and Beppe ensured it was a happy occasion for everyone. But the happiest moments came a few days later when news reached us that Lina and Brunati had been freed.

* * *

The new year brought a resumption of activities at the villa. Various members of the resistance paid visits to consult Beppe or collect such things as food and blankets deposited there – some even stayed the night. George and I became increasingly apprehensive about these comings and goings. If the suspicions of the authorities were ever aroused and they decided to call and check, the discovery of British officers would have unthinkable consequences for the family. We had already spent three weeks at Llo di Mare and decided it was time to move.

By chance, it was just then that Lina and Brunati finally put in an appearance, so we made preparations to go off together. Baiardo was our objective. As far as we knew, it was still a safe place, although we had had no news from there since we left before Christmas. Lina and Brunati had not been back since their release.

It was a great disappointment to be retracing our steps back to our old haunts. One felt very sorry for the boys whose valiant efforts in setting up the Corsica venture had been frustrated by bad luck. But we could at least be thankful that no harm had come to all these brave people who had risked so much to help us.

* * *

At dawn the next day we passed through Negi, and being well clear of roads and villages we were able to continue on our way to Baiardo in broad daylight. Negotiating rough mountain tracks was no longer the problem it had been at night. It turned into a beautiful day and it felt good to be out in the fresh air again enjoying the sights of nature, especially the distant snow-capped peaks and the mimosa trees dotted around the valleys.

That evening, we were in the neighbourhood of Baiardo, but before proceeding to the hut beyond the village we looked in at Lina's villa. We were due for a shock. The place had been thoroughly ransacked – no doubt the work of Fascists. It was a complete shambles; glass and china had been smashed, sheets, blankets and clothing stolen, mattresses ripped open with their contents strewn around and beds broken. Even the kitchen stove had been removed.

If Lina was distressed, she did not show it. Silently, we continued on our way to the country hut, wondering if it had suffered the same fate. Fortunately, it had not. All was well, and the few partisans still there had not been disturbed.

While the hut was proving a good refuge, it was, of course, remote from sources of supplies and also from friends who could keep one informed of the situation elsewhere – always important. For these reasons there was constant movement among the group. George and I had nowhere else to go so stayed put.

* * *

After a few days, Lina and Brunati left for San Remo as there were some matters they wished to attend to. Despite earlier setbacks, they had not entirely given up hope of finding some means of getting us to Corsica or of finding a guide to help us cross the frontier into France.

While they were away, the Porcheddu family bravely made the long journey to Baiardo to bring food. They stayed overnight in the village and returned to Arziglia the next day. Then a week later, Beppe and Rita were back but this time bringing the sad news that Lina and Brunati had been rearrested.

Beppe's main object in coming to see us again was to propose that we return secretly to Llo di Mare and hide there until we decided what to do. Winter had overtaken us, making journeying over mountainous country difficult, while the future at Baiardo was uncertain now with the loss of Lina and Brunati. Llo di Mare would be a way out, but we were unhappy about putting the onus on Beppe again. He argued that providing absolutely no one – not even trusted friends – was aware of this plan, then there could be no danger of anything ever coming to the knowledge of the authorities.

We discussed the matter, sitting under an olive tree out of earshot of the hut. Before Beppe left, it was agreed that four days later we would return to the villa.

* * *

The next day, we made it known to the two remaining occupants of the hut that, failing the release of Lina and Brunati and their return to Baiardo within the next few days, we would have to push on into France as originally planned, guide or no guide.

Three days later, having, I believe, thoroughly convinced our friends of our stated intentions, we were ready to leave. They pressed on us much of the remains of the precious food store. The younger of the two, a boy of sixteen, cried as he embraced us and said goodbye. It was sad to deceive them like this; they had been loyal comrades. But with so much at stake, security considerations were paramount. Hopefully, after our departure, the word would get around that the '*Inglesi*' had gone to France, and we would be forgotten.

The light was fading as we set off westwards towards the frontier. We continued until it was dark and we were well clear of the area. Then we changed direction and headed south for the coast and Bordighera.

Chapter 18

Refuge in 'Llo Di Mare' – a Riviera Villa

L lo di Mare was the classical Riviera villa: white walls, green shutters, red tiled roof, balustrated balcony on the first floor and a terracotta terrace beneath arches on the ground floor. It was separated from the main road by a walled garden clustered with palms, cypress and fir trees. Roaming freely in the grounds was a huge black Newfoundland dog called Marte, posing an apparent threat to all strangers; they were not to guess that he was, in fact, as gentle as a lamb. The building faced south, overlooking the sea, with wooded hills and mountains behind. The beach was a stone's throw away but separated from the villa by the main road and railway running parallel to the coast.

George and I occupied a large bedroom upstairs with a balcony looking down on the front garden and the road. The windows had latticed shutters, through which we could peer at and observe the outside world unseen. We remained indoors during the day, of course, but were able to exercise in the well-concealed garden after nightfall.

The family followed a regular daily routine, undisturbed by our presence. Beppe ensured that the girls and Bitita, although over school age, continued their education at home under his supervision. Mornings were devoted to academic studies, while afternoons were taken up by piano practice for the girls – there were two pianos – and violin practice for Bitita. Evenings were free, but Giovanna and Ninilla made few excursions from the house, especially now that it was winter. The war and the German occupation deprived young people of many of the social activities they could otherwise have enjoyed. Fortunately, the home contained a vast library of interesting books in several languages and a wide selection of classical music records; all were constantly in use.

Rita would be out most mornings to shop and so on, but Beppe, partly because of his disability, rarely ventured beyond the garden and spent most days at home. Following a short gymnastics session and lessons for his children, he would set them work and then apply himself to drawing and painting in his studio. He was thus able to keep a tight rein on everything. Now and then he himself might turn to the violin for diversion, but happily not too often; he did not have the delicate touch of his young son.

Lunch and dinner were the two occasions of the day when we would sit down together with the whole family and enjoy their company. These were happy, light-hearted times, and Beppe's conversation, especially, was always interesting and entertaining. Normally he was serious-minded and reserved, but at the table he relaxed and would often be very amusing; then his eyes would light up and a broad smile spread across his face, revealing his prominent teeth. But there were also times when we would experience a trough instead of a peak in his artistic temperament; then a deep depression would descend on everyone and everything. Luckily, these occasions were rare!

Rita, by comparison, was even-tempered and invariably good-humoured. A ready smile adorned a face of fine classical features, with dark hair brushed back and tied neatly in a bun. She contended bravely with the task of feeding us all. It was not easy. Official rations were totally inadequate, which meant that people were virtually dependent on a variable black market. Having two extra guests in the house did not exactly help. There had been a domestic servant, but she had left shortly before our arrival and now, for obvious reasons of security, was not to be replaced.

We considered ourselves very fortunate to have been given refuge with such a happy, well disciplined family. By good chance, too, both Giovanna and Ninilla had a good command of English, thanks to a pre-war American governess. They were also fluent in German and French, the family having lived in the Tyrol and in France. Their facility for languages had been developed by Beppe's constant tutelage and the strict rule that they were never to speak Italian when at home. In practice, this came to mean whenever their father was at home.

* * *

Visits to the villa by members of the Resistance had almost ceased since the arrest of Brunati, but one day an ex-Baiardo partisan who had known George and myself called on Beppe. He brought the tragic news that two British officers had been caught on the French/Italian border and shot. Believing that we had already left for France, he was speculating on the possibility of it being us. Beppe, of course, resisted the temptation to allay his fears.

It was the sort of pretence that had to be maintained. No one, in any circumstances, could be taken into confidence about us. Not a single person outside the family knew of our present whereabouts, and it had to be kept that way.

* * *

Beppe, for political reasons, had isolated himself from much of the community around him and rarely indulged in social activities. The few friends who came to see him were usually intellectuals like himself who shared his ideals. One was Padre Pelloux, a much respected local priest – he also tutored the girls in philosophy. Beppe enjoyed his and others' visits for the mental stimulus provided by the long and often heated discussions which ensued. These callers posed no problem for us. They remained downstairs, while we kept out of the way in our refuge upstairs.

It was not so simple, however, when members of the younger generation called at the villa. They tended to roam about and expected to spend much of the time in the rooms of Bitita and the girls upstairs. We remained shut in our room with the door locked whenever they showed up.

While casual visits from young people were not normally encouraged, we decided on one occasion to turn their natural inquisitiveness to our advantage. Our plan was to have a group of these talkative friends invited for the afternoon, prior to which George and I would disappear altogether. They would then have free run of all the rooms in the villa which would demonstrate in the best possible way the normality of life at Llo di Mare.

On the appointed day George and I moved out to an empty stable in a walled compound at the rear of the house. Here we were able to lock ourselves in well out of sight. The compound itself was overgrown and never used. Access to it was through a side gate, which was always locked. In the event, it proved a very successful afternoon and all went according to plan. It was 'grist to the mill'.

Later on, the stable was to serve us again but in a more serious, sinister situation. It was fortuitous, therefore, that the original occupant, a small pony called Dora, had been despatched to Piedmont some six months earlier. She had been a great favourite of the family and the source of much amusement to local children when she and Marte, the Newfoundland, chased each other around the front garden.

* * *

Living in the privacy of a villa afforded us the priceless benefit of having constant access to the radio. The daily broadcasts in English from London enabled us to keep abreast of the war situation. Rita had her own radio and was also an avid listener. She spent most evenings tuned into the local broadcasts so was able to keep us all informed on what the Germans and Fascists were saying too.

We were more than well catered for in terms of world news coverage, but less well informed about important matters of local concern. For example, we had had no news whatever about Lena and Brunati since their arrest two months earlier. We felt it likely that they had been sent to labour camps, possibly in Germany. Of Vincenzo and Federico, our collaborators in the abortive attempt to reach Corsica, we knew only that they were no longer in Bordighera. In fact, contact with local members of the Resistance had now been virtually lost. It was only on the radio that we occasionally heard of partisan exploits and German reprisals occurring elsewhere in northern Italy. But any idea that on the Riviera we were somewhat remote from these conflicts was quickly dispelled when one morning we were suddenly plunged into the realities of war right there on our own doorstep.

* * *

It was barely light when the sudden thunder and vibrations of nearby gunfire shook the building and woke the household. It continued intermittently for fifteen minutes and then ceased. We concluded it was some local artillery unit indulging in firing practice. Later in the day, however, we learned that it had been in earnest. German guns had been firing on a mountain village called Seborga – close to our old lair at Negi. The village had been suspected of harbouring partisans. The Germans surrounded the place and when the barrage lifted, went in. Five persons accused of being partisans were dragged out into the square and shot. Two of the five, we learned later, had been young women and former school acquaintances of Giovanna and Ninilla.

* * *

We needed no reminder of the ever present threat from the enemy around us. Wherever we were we made contingency plans to meet it as best we could. Here in Llo di Mare the obvious danger was from an unannounced visit by the police. Attempting to escape from the house in such circumstances would certainly incur the risk of discovery. The only alternative was concealment indoors. By good fortune there was an almost perfect hiding place exactly where we needed it – in our own bedroom.

Tucked away in one corner of our room was a narrow door giving access to a tiny box room about a metre square. It was an unusual adjunct to a room. To one side of this door stood a tall double wardrobe which, when pushed into the corner, completely concealed the entrance to the box room. With the wardrobe in this position, a stranger to the bedroom would have no reason to suspect the existence of anything behind it.

In an emergency we would need a few moments to get into the box room, and then the wardrobe would have to be pushed into position. Normally there would be time enough for this, as the garden gates were always kept locked, which would give a breathing space between someone ringing the bell and actually being admitted. On trying it out we found, also, that it needed only one person to slide the wardrobe across.

Inside the box room we added a refinement in the form of a panel of shelves. From inside we could swing it round like a second door, filling the entrance and concealing what was behind it. Anyone opening the outside door would then be confronted with just a shallow cupboard of bookshelves. This could be crucial in the event of intruders forcing an entry into the villa at a time when everyone might be out with no one to move the wardrobe.

So often one takes the most elaborate precautions in the interests of security, only to find in the end that they were unnecessary. Not so our little corner box room. It was soon put to the test.

* * *

It happened one dull, rainy afternoon. Beppe and Rita were taking their siesta; the others were out. The bell at the front gate rang. I peered out of the window at a safe distance and saw a car parked on the road outside the gate. Two men – strangers – in raincoats and broad-brimmed trilby hats were waiting to come in. Almost immediately, Beppe was up and into our room, pale-faced and serious. Words were not spoken. In a matter of seconds we were closeted in the box room with the wardrobe in place.

Moments later, voices could be heard in the hallway as the visitors were let in. They must have entered one of the reception rooms as we heard a door close but nothing else. George and I waited in silence.

Ten minutes passed, and there were voices again, followed by the dreaded sound of footsteps on the stairs. They were coming up. I held my breath and froze on the spot as they came directly into our room. I could hear them moving about and talking but could not make out what was being said. Then they left and wandered, presumably, into the other bedrooms and out of earshot. We breathed a little more easily when finally we heard them descending the stairs and departing.

On release from our refuge we learned that these men were, indeed, police and from the headquarters in Imperia, the provincial capital. They had questioned Beppe about alleged involvement with the underground movement and with British officers. Beppe, of course, refuted all their allegations. They then searched the house as well as conducting a cursory examination of his papers. Nothing incriminating was found. Nevertheless, before departing, they told Beppe to consider himself under house arrest and to report to police headquarters at Imperia in two days' time.

Two anxious days dragged past, and then Beppe and Rita left home in a horse-drawn carriage taking them to the station at Bordighera for the train to Imperia. Rita invariably accompanied Beppe on outside excursions as, apart from anything else, he needed help when out walking because of his handicap. The family put a brave face on everything, but the departure from home that morning was certainly a sombre moment.

Another long twenty-four hours went by, and then at midday a carriage drew up outside the gate. To our tremendous relief it was Beppe and Rita. The children rushed out to meet them and they all walked back to the house arm in arm.

* * *

The outcome of their attendance at the Police Headquarters was that Beppe had been cleared and was no longer under house arrest. Nevertheless, it had been a painful experience for him, especially being unexpectedly confronted by his old friend Brunati. We had not known that Brunati was being held at Imperia. While they were together, Brunati had indicated to Beppe that he had given nothing away and had not implicated him in any way. Unfortunately, in the past, Brunati had been less than cautious about his own anti-Fascist activities, so the police had evidence enough against him. Beppe denied all the allegations, and the charges against him were eventually dropped, at least for the time being.

Despite the reprieve, the whole ugly business had cast a dark shadow over everyone and everything. Yet, by a twist of fate, an unexpected bonus had emerged which promised some assurance for Beppe's future. It arose from his making the acquaintance of a senior police officer called Palmero.

* * *

Palmero had been responsible for investigating Beppe and had subjected him to a somewhat lengthy interrogation. When it was all over and Beppe had been released unconditionally, they parted on quite friendly terms, or so Palmero believed. He said he would like to call on Beppe for a further talk, just to clear up one or two matters, and a date was fixed for his visit to Llo di Mare.

On the appointed day George and I withdrew in good time to the stable behind the house as on a previous occasion. We remained there until evening, when Bitita called to say that all was clear – the guest had come and gone.

That night at supper, the story of the Palmero visit was related, to much amusement. He had arrived in a good humour, plainly intent on making it a friendly social occasion. The family had responded by being courteous and making the visitor feel welcome. He seemed very 'taken' by Beppe and his reminiscences, but apparently even more so by his very attractive daughters. Before leaving he said he would like to come again and was particularly keen, he said, to see Giovanna and Ninilla perform the classical dance duets which they had recently done for charity with great success at the San Remo Casino Theatre. Assured of the family's further hospitality, he took fond farewells of everyone and left in high spirits. On departure, he had hinted to Beppe that he would see to it that he was not troubled by the authorities in future.

In truth, the visit had been something of an ordeal. They had found Palmero quite odious, a poor ignoramus who had obviously relished demonstrating his influence and authority over a well-bred, educated family.

It must have gone against the grain for Beppe to have shown politeness and civility to a Fascist official; it was probably the first time in his life that he had done so. But he realized the necessity, at times like this, of behaving tactfuly with individuals like Palmero. He knew, too, that Palmero, and others of his kind who were cooperating with the Germans, could foresee the day when they themselves might be seeking ways of saving their own skins. Men such as Beppe could be influential in the post-war period.

* * *

One day, George developed an agonisingly painful toothache. Now, for security reasons, we had prayed that the need for medical help would never arise. Unfortunately, George's pain worsened, and Beppe decided something must be done. A dentist in San Remo named Dr Ronga, known to have no love for Fascists, was contacted by Rita. She asked him if he would perform an extraction, urgently needed, on a British Army officer at that moment operating with Italian partisans in the mountains nearby. She said a rendezvous could be arranged at Llo di Mare, if convenient, and the officer brought down. Dr Ronga agreed everything and an appointment was made.

All went according to plan and George was relieved of a large abscess. Meanwhile, I kept out of the way. The dentist learned nothing more about the patient than what he had already been told by Rita. He was unlikely to speak elsewhere about what he had done because of the obvious danger to himself.

* * *

As if the Porcheddu family had not enough to contend with already, yet another burden was about to descend upon the household. One morning, quite out of the blue, two ladies appeared on the doorstep seeking a short period of refuge. They were the wife and daughter of Concetto Marchesi, Rector of Padova University and an old friend of the family. For a long time he had been an outspoken critic of Fascism, but now the authorities were after him. He had gone underground, and his wife and daughter thought it wise to follow suit. Beppe and Rita took them in without hesitation.

We now had real problems. If any outsider, no matter who, ever learned about us, our present solid security would be compromised and we should have to leave. On the other hand, attempting to avoid all contact with the newcomers, who would be living under the same roof and, like ourselves, never venturing outside, would be fraught with difficulty. But Beppe insisted the situation could be handled.

* * *

So nothing was said to the ladies about our presence, and they settled comfortably into the downstairs sitting room, which was set aside for their sole use, including for sleeping. It contained a grand piano, much to the delight of the daughter, who was a professional concert pianist and a great exponent of Chopin. Unluckily, our bedroom was immediately above them, so as well as locking ourselves in we had to discard all footwear and speak only in whispers. Meals were smuggled up to us while someone occupied the attention of the ladies downstairs. Similar arrangements were made for our excursions to the bathroom.

This bizarre situation endured for the two weeks the ladies were in the house, and it is incredible to think we succeeded in deceiving them completely at such close range and for so long. There was, however, just one anxious moment, when unexpected footsteps on the stairs one evening forced me to closet myself quickly in a wardrobe in the girls' room seconds before the older lady entered.

It was something of a relief when the visitors finally departed and life at Llo di Mare returned to normal – if one could ever call it that. A break from Chopin, too, was not unwelcome.

* * *

In these days the burning question on all our minds was where and when the second front would open. We had been at Llo di Mare for three months and every day we had listened assiduously to the broadcasts from Radio London, anxiously hoping for the answer. Finally, one morning it came. Over the air flashed the message, 'Allied troops land in Normandy.' It was June 1944.

This was wonderful news and a tremendous boost to morale. A landing in the English Channel area had been expected but, perhaps optimistically, we had argued that a beachhead established at the same time on the Riviera would assist any front in western Europe as well as helping to revive the stalemate on the southern Italian front. So we could not help feeling some disappointment that nothing seemed to be happening in the Mediterranean area. Anyway, things were now on the move, and we all took heart.

We kept a constant watch on the road outside, where there was unmistakable evidence of an intensification of military preparations. Convoys, both motorized and horse-drawn, passed by frequently. An armoured train appeared and started patrolling up and down the coastal railway. Beach defences along these parts of the Riviera were also being strengthened. This we learned from Bitita who, for his own good, had sought employment as an interpreter with the German Todt Organization (a civil and military engineering group) engaged on these works.

The Allies, too, were becoming more active in these parts, at least in the air and by sea. Aircraft appeared for the first time and attacked targets along the coast after dark. The bombings were close enough one night to force us to vacate the house and seek the sanctuary of the garden. This prompted George and I to start on the construction of a trench. For several nights we went to work, digging in a concealed part of the garden until we made one large enough to hold us all in the event of renewed danger. Such an occasion was not long in coming.

* * *

A few evenings later, as we were preparing for bed, there was the most shattering explosion I had ever heard. I thought a bomb had fallen in the garden. The villa shook with the impact and glass flew in all directions. In no time we were all downstairs, outside and into the trench. We crouched down wondering what would follow, but nothing did. We could not understand it as there was no sound of aircraft or anything else.

It was not until the next morning that we learned what had happened. It was reported that an Allied submarine had fired a torpedo at a passing German ship but missed the target. The torpedo had careered on and landed on the beach at Arziglia, virtually outside Llo di Mare. A blackened area on the stony foreshore and the remains of a projectile marked the spot. The high sea wall must have taken most of the blast, but the villas nearby suffered broken windows, while ours sustained a long crack in the front wall facing the sea.

* * *

It became clear from their continuing preparations for military action that the Germans were taking the threat of an Allied landing in these parts seriously. Reinforcements of men and materials were arriving in the locality, and soldiers were being billeted in various places, including the old casino near Arziglia which we could see from the house.

Uniformed German soldiers had become a familiar sight passing along the road outside. One late afternoon, however, on hearing the door bell ring and taking a casual glance through the window, we got more than a shock to find two of them standing at the gate waiting to come in. Marte was delivering the usual noisy welcome reserved for strangers. George and I disappeared into the box room and the wardrobe was moved into position.

Soon we heard the visitors being admitted to the house, and before long they were tramping up the stairs, somewhat heavy-footedly. On reaching the landing they came straight into our room. I felt cold. We could hear the girls conversing with them in German. What did these men want? At least there was no attempt to pull the place apart. It was a strange feeling to be penned in there so close to enemy soldiers and quite helpless. Moments later, they left the room and descended the stairs. The noise of the front door closing soon afterwards meant they had gone.

The high-spirited voices of the family scampering up the stairs to release us signalled that the danger had passed. We were relieved to learn that there had been nothing sinister about their visit.

The soldiers had simply been on a foraging mission, hoping to appropriate suitable household articles to furnish their new quarters. In the event, they had taken nothing, not even some items Beppe suggested they might find useful. Perhaps they felt the situation embarrassing, especially as they had been addressed in their own tongue. They had acted most properly and left empty-handed.

* * *

Despite what seemed to us signs of an imminent invasion, it was to be another two months before the great event actually occurred. It was the height of the summer season – 15 August. At other times the Riviera would have been welcoming crowds of happy holidaymakers. Today, an Allied armada was approaching and landing thousands of soldiers on the beaches between Cannes and San Tropez to a hostile reception from German guns.

From where we were we could catch the distant sounds but not the sight of battle. It was not long, however, before Allied warships appeared on the horizon and could be seen shelling enemy positions along the coast. Within the week, a radio announcement confirmed that the Allied landings in the Mediterranean had been successful and that a fresh beachhead had been firmly established. This one was 50 miles from Bordighera. Our spirits rose.

With our own troops so close, the prospect of an early liberation was real. Each day we waited and watched eagerly for any news or sign of the front moving this way. But the hoped-for quick advance into these parts did not materialize. As the weeks passed, there was some progress in this direction, but the main thrust was developing northwards into France, presumably to link up with operations in Normandy.

Nonetheless, the Allied pressure on the enemy here, entrenched in depth along the French-Italian frontier, was maintained both by naval guns at sea and land-based artillery. As the Allies edged a little closer to us and occupied Monte Carlo, places like Ventimiglia, a frontier town in Italy still in German hands, and even Bordighera, came increasingly under fire. Our sorties to the safety of the trench became more frequent.

The intermittent bombardment, though not intense, was nevertheless causing enough damage and casualties to prompt the authorities to make available the local railway tunnels as air-raid shelters. Train services by this time had ceased altogether. For a while Beppe and family left home in the evenings with their sleeping bags and reading material to spend the night in the nearest tunnel. But these places proved crowded and stuffy, making it far from easy to sleep. In the mornings they would drag themselves back to the villa with tired, drawn faces, exhausted and ready for bed.

One night in the shelter, the girls got into conversation with a young German soldier and invited him to the villa. He was a gentle soul, by all accounts, very homesick and grateful for the hospitality. He visited the villa several times when off duty and liked to browse through the German books, of which there were many in the library below our room. What interested us most, of course, was whether in the course of conversation with the girls he would give any indication of his unit moving away from this area. Regrettably, he did not.

* * *

Whilst important military gains were being reported daily from the rest of Europe, the situation in these parts remained unchanged. As autumn gave way to winter, the routine exchange of gunfire continued as before, but there was still no sign of an Allied attempt to break through. George and I kept a hopeful watch on the road outside for any evidence of an enemy withdrawal, but we were always disappointed.

With the approach of the new year, we could not help feeling frustrated at finding ourselves still on the wrong side of the line, having had such high hopes following the local landings a few months earlier. Those heady days when the joys of sharing the moments of liberation with the family seemed imminent were now just a memory. A sort of resignation had set in, and even Beppe was showing signs of impatience. But far worse was to follow. Information leaked from the local authorities warned of a sudden, tragic turn of events, which shattered the serenity of the home and brought about a sharp and bitter end to all our hopes and prayers.

* * *

It came about when a trusted friend of the family, who worked in the Bordighera municipal offices, called at the villa to see Beppe. He brought news that he had just seen a secret list of names of persons earmarked for future arrest as hostages. Heading the list was the name 'Giuseppe Porcheddu'. There was now only one course of action – Beppe must disappear, and quickly.

No time was lost in evacuating Llo di Mare. George and I left that night; Beppe, Rita and Bitita fled to the home of Luigi, next door to Brunati's villa, half a mile along the coast; Giovanna and Ninilla sought refuge with old family friends called Pazielli. They lived in a large mansion, very remote and situated in extensive grounds, high up on a wooded hill overlooking Bordighera.

* * *

It was a big wrench leaving the family after all this time, but especially leaving them in such circumstances. We had grown close, sharing common hopes and ideals, in the defence of which they had accepted grave personal risks. They were a unique family. Beppe's strict moral code permeated the whole household, and like many such regulated, disciplined homes, it was a very happy one. Rita was his perfect counterpart, her invariable cheerfulness and good humour creating a relaxed atmosphere. Her relationship with her daughters was particularly close. She did not share the intellectual pursuits of the others but she was tireless in providing for the material needs of us all.

* * *

Our presence in the house had, among other things, curtailed the hospitality which the family, and especially Giovanna and Ninilla, would normally have extended to their friends outside. Attractive girls, they were much sought after. They still enjoyed limited social activities away from the house but spent more time than usual at home. Whilst at home, Beppe ensured that the girls, as well as Bitita, were well occupied with their studies and music. These activities, together with their natural high spirits, enabled them to adjust to these restrictions.

We, of course, were only too glad of their company, which was always gay and refreshing. Indeed, our days with the family had been almost always cheerful and sunny, and time had passed surprisingly quickly for us. Our constant dream had been the safe delivery of the family from these anxious times and the joy of celebrating liberation with them. Sadly, it was now not to be. I think that only people who have lived through such a hostile environment and a dangerous occupation can really understand the depth of underlying fear and despair and appreciate the immense relief of deliverance when it comes.

* * *

That last night, after bidding farewell to Beppe and Rita – the girls and Bitita had already left – George and I crept out of the villa and made straight for the safety of the hills immediately behind. When high up, we sat down to rest for a moment and gazed down at the bay of Arziglia while eating salami sandwiches hastily prepared by Rita. Through the misty darkness we took our last look at Llo di Mare, now barely visible.

My feelings, shared I know by George, were a mixture of sadness at parting, regret at the failure of achieving a happy ending for the family after all they had done for us, and yet thanks that our long association with them still remained a secret and had, so far at least, brought them no harm. But, in my case, I was troubled by a more personal emotion; I had fallen in love with Giovanna. I did not know whether my sentiments were reciprocated or not, although there were times when I thought I detected a mutual regard. From the beginning, Giovanna was fully aware of my commitment to someone else, and that still stood. In any case, she herself had a longstanding attachment to a young man, but he had left Italy the previous year and gone with his family to live temporarily in Switzerland.

It had to be recognized that these were times of great uncertainty and danger; one could live only by the day and hope for the morrow. We had been thrown together in exceptional circumstances, and it could only be later on, when things returned to normality, that such personal relationships could take their proper place and the emotions aroused by them find their own level.

George and I sat in silence finishing our sandwiches. We then stirred ourselves, turned our backs on the coast and headed north for the mountains.

Villa Llo Di Mare, painted by the author in 1996. (*Ross Family Archive*)

Chapter 19

At Large with Partisans

By the next morning we were high up at the top end of the valley close to our old haunt of Negi. Previously, when hiding there, we had the support of Federico, Vincenzo and Elio, but they, like all the others we had known, had long since left. Nevertheless, we were still hopeful of contacting partisans somewhere in these parts. We had heard various rumours about their activities but had no positive information about them or their location. Unfortunately, Beppe was now no longer in direct touch with members of the resistance, and in any case there had been no time to make enquiries on our behalf. It was a case of just striking out on our own, hoping we would meet up with them.

Our old Negi hideout was deserted, so we decided to investigate the other buildings scattered around. To save time on this, we split up and arranged to meet an hour later. I duly set off along one of the terraces, enjoying the fresh country air of a sunny morning and with a feeling almost of regained freedom.

* * *

While strolling along I was running my eyes over a row of vines on the terrace immediately above me when suddenly I was struck dumb by the sight of a German soldier standing motionless, staring down the valley, rifle slung on his shoulder, partly hidden among the leafless vines. He must have seen me already, long before I had spotted him. There was nothing for it but to brazen it out. I continued on with bowed head and feigning a slight limp. Passing immediately below him, I glanced up casually for a second. He was still gazing unconcernedly down the valley. I went on without looking back. There was no challenge; thankfully, he had chosen to ignore me.

It was a numbing experience to have been so close to recapture only hours after leaving the security of the villa. In previous times not even a policeman had been seen in these remote parts; now the German army itself was in occupation. It was a sobering thought. The proximity of the new front meant that the enemy could be anywhere around now, and we should have to exercise ever greater care. We decided to press on northwards as quickly as possible, avoiding all contact for the time being.

On our way we looked in at the old stone hut at Baiardo but found it deserted. We were disappointed but not surprised, and kept on. Further afield, in what we reckoned was a safer area, we sought food once more from the local people. These good country folk were, as always, ready to help, but we became conscious of changes in their attitude. Generally, they seemed weary and more suspicious of strangers than before. Offers of accommodation for the night in haylofts were not so readily forthcoming. The alternative was sleeping rough, which in midwinter meant contending with cold and damp. George and I joked together about the recently forsaken luxuries of Llo di Mare.

* * *

By the fifth day we were 15 miles inland, having reached the foothills of Monte Ceppo, but had still not succeeded in finding partisans. We began to wonder if we ever would. Then, in the late afternoon, we were following a path through a wood when suddenly a young man in plain clothes sprang out from the undergrowth where he had been hiding and stood in our path facing us. He was brandishing a pistol and pointed it straight at us. He called on us in Italian to halt and raise our hands. We attempted to explain ourselves, but he was taking no chances and, still keeping us covered, ordered us to proceed along the path until finally we emerged from the wood. Not far away was an old farm building, to which he directed us. On arrival, he ushered us inside. In a semi-dark room was a group of ten men or so sitting around the remains of a log fire. They were variously dressed in old clothes but each one wore a distinctive red scarf tied in a knot around his neck. To our great relief, we knew that at long last we had found our partisans.

* * *

Our joy, however, was not shared by those around us. One of them, obviously the leader, fat, with shifty eyes and a large revolver stuck in his belt, scrutinized us closely and fired a barrage of questions at us. Who were we? Where did we come from? What did we want? Who were our friends? And so on. To our despair, they were dissatisfied with our attempts, in our limited Italian, to explain our background and establish our identity. It soon dawned on us that at the back of their minds was the suspicion that we might be Germans attempting to pass ourselves off as British! Apparently, it had been done before. What was clearly irking them was our flat refusal to divulge anything about the family with whom we claimed to have been living for the past nine months. The protection of the family was our first concern, and we had no intention whatever of exposing them to the smallest danger by identifying them to men like these, who were themselves in constant fear of capture and all that might follow. Partisans were being continually hunted down by the Germans and Fascists, and it was well known that if taken prisoner they would be subjected to intensive interrogation and often executed afterwards. If they were not in possession of such information, then they could do no harm. Strangely, it was not possible to make them understand and accept this. Our relations with the group, or at least with their leader, turned sour.

We had not anticipated this kind of reception. It was uncomfortable and embarrassing. The leader, called Bruno, ensured that we were kept under constant surveillance, night and day. He himself rarely spoke to us. We soon took an intense dislike to him. He was loud-mouthed, arrogant and boastful. It was claimed that he had, in the past, executed five captured enemy by shooting them. We did not trust him.

The unit under Bruno's command numbered about twenty-five and formed part of the Garibaldi Partisan Brigade. Further north, we learned, the partisan units belonged to the Badoglio Brigade. They all, of course, had a common enemy, but internally there were political differences. Our Garibaldini were avowed Communists – hence the red scarves.

* * *

On our third day with them it was decided the unit should change location. After a day's long march we halted at a large disused farmhouse.

Sentries were posted, while the rest of us settled down in a large loft for the night. Bruno and three of his henchmen, we noted, went off separately – apparently to pay a social call at a nearby farm.

About midnight, the four of them got back, stumbled up to the loft in the darkness, the worse for drink, and slumped down at the far end of the room. George and I had lain awake some time. He nudged me when it became apparent from their muffled talk that they were discussing us. One suggested that there were plenty of Germans who had lived in South Africa and now spoke fluent English. Finally, matters were concluded by Bruno, who said that tomorrow he would shoot us if we still refused to tell them everything. For the rest of the night I lay awake listening to their snoring and contemplating the approach of dawn.

* * *

When morning came, the usual routine was played out: men rousing themselves, cursing, disappearing outside and then returning, lighting cigarettes, coughing, spitting, searching for lice in their clothing or sharing out the remnants of the previous day's food. George and I got up without talking and together descended the steps of the loft to emerge into the courtyard outside. It was a clear, chilly winter's morning. Groups had gathered in the yard outside, unusually silent. Bruno was already up and talking with a stranger. On seeing us, the two of them immediately came over. The newcomer introduced himself, saying his name was Vittò and that he commanded a large partisan unit elsewhere in the area. He said there were two Americans with his group and that they would wish to meet us. The idea, obviously, was that they should interrogate us and decide whether or not we were what we claimed to be. We could hardly believe our good fortune. It was a God-sent opportunity for clearing up the doubts over us once and for all.

The arrival of Vittò that morning was quite fortuitous; he just happened to be passing that way and called in. It was an unexpected twist of fate that changed everything. Whatever plans Bruno may have had were now forestalled. Whether the previous night's threat was serious or just the ramblings of a drunken man was never, thankfully, put to the test. I need hardly describe the relief of setting off for new territory under the wing of Vittò and out of the clutches of Bruno. However, we were not yet rid of him entirely as he decided to tag along. He was still his surly self, and we trusted him no more than before.

* * *

A party of ten of us set off for Vittò's outfit. The going was rough, with patches of snow here and there, while the weather worsened. They said it would take us two days. It became misty and damp. George was suffering from stomach cramps and had difficulty keeping up when on the march. But he did not complain – illness was something to be endured and there was simply no medical aid.

The first night brought us to a remote village, high up and well out of range of surprise enemy attack. We received a royal welcome from the villagers. Young men were no longer to be found in these rural communities. They had been either called up for service or were more likely on the run, hoping to avoid it, far from home. Our unexpected arrival, therefore, was an occasion for rejoicing especially on the part of the young women. We were led to one of the buildings and gathered together in a large room, where a welcome wood fire was soon blazing. But even more welcome were the plates of hot, steaming spaghetti brought in by a procession of local housewives. Morale climbed higher as the younger girls appeared and joined in the feasting and drinking. Soon a chorus of patriotic songs adopted by the partisans was to be heard above the lively chatter and laughter.

As the celebrations drew to a close, most of the girls paired off with men and disappeared elsewhere for the night. I noticed that Vittò, who had now assumed responsibility for us, could not be persuaded to retire with a young woman, despite her pleadings, and instead stuck manfully to his guns, taking George and myself off to a hayloft for the night where he could keep an eye on us.

* * *

We reached Vittò's units the following day after trekking cautiously over some 10 miles of difficult country. His men were scattered around, high up in a mountainous region above the small town of Montaldo. George and I were shown to a stone hut occupied by the two Americans. They turned out to be sergeant pilots who had parachuted to safety when their planes had been shot down some months before. They were known to the partisans as 'Ricky' and 'Reg'.

It needed only a short interview for them to assure Vittò that we were indeed genuine British officers. They appreciated our point about protecting the name of anyone who had helped us. So at long last we were accepted as partisans. Now we could feel free and act freely. As for Bruno, we saw nothing more of him. He must have made his way back to his own unit, perhaps disappointed.

* * *

We soon came to realize how totally desperate the situation really was for these partisans. They were critically short of arms, so offensive operations were virtually impossible. No place could be called safe, so it was essential to keep on the move. This meant there could be no certainty of shelter at night or of food by day. Limited funds filtering down to us helped pay for supplies from local farmers. Most of them were trustworthy, despite threats of enemy reprisals, but there were a few who privately cursed the partisans. These could be a source of danger. Informers on both sides played a vital, often fatal, part in the conflict.

Our ranks contained men from all walks of life. The majority had left home to avoid military service with the Germans, but not all were young. Some were political refugees, actively opposed to Fascism and prepared to take up arms against it. All were now banded together and, despite their miserable plight, were disciplined, determined and patriotic.

* * *

The one-time safe areas controlled by partisans where supplies could be dropped by air were a thing of the past. The enemy had free rein everywhere, and the struggle had become one-sided. The Germans had bases from which to operate and unlimited transport, arms and supplies, whereas the partisans had none of these things. Nevertheless, just the presence of partisans posed a threat which obliged the enemy to commit not inconsiderable forces permanently to anti-partisan operations. Italians of the Fascist Black Brigade as well as Germans were employed on these missions. The former were particularly hated, and no mercy was shown to any who fell into our hands.

Enemy operations followed a set pattern. A specific area would be selected where they believed partisans to be hiding. They would make their approach before dawn, surround the place and then move in at first light in large numbers and systematically comb it out. Machine guns mounted on high points overlooking the search area would open fire on anyone spotted running for it. In a few hours it would all be over, and the enemy would withdraw back to the safety of their barracks in town. This type of early morning raid was known as *rastrellamento,* or raking over. It was the partisans' nightmare, and their only defence was to attempt to confuse the enemy by frequent changes of location.

* * *

Our new group seemed better organized than the previous one. Their position was more secure, being further inland in mountainous territory and remote from main roads and towns, but like the others, they were seriously short of arms. However, within a week of our joining them there was a sudden prospect of everything changing.

A British Special Service officer unexpectedly arrived on the scene, having landed by sea nearby. His mission was to arrange a delivery of arms and supplies to the partisans and he was equipped with a radio and an operator, so was able to keep in touch and exchange information with his HQ in Nice.

His name was Captain Robert Bentley. We met him only briefly as he was constantly on the move. It was unsafe for him to transmit radio messages from the same place too often because of the risk of detection by the Germans. Apparently, they were already aware of his activities and were out looking for him.

He explained to us that the plan was for a submarine's rubber dinghies to land the equipment at night on the beach at Arma di Taggia – the nearest suitable point on the coast. At the same time, the returning dinghies could transport the Americans and ourselves out to the submarine, so enabling us to escape from enemy territory and rejoin our own forces. The landings were scheduled for a moonless night two weeks later.

* * *

Meanwhile, our little group of four Allied officers was increased to six by the arrival of two more Americans – flight lieutenants named Erickson and Klemme, recently shot down. They had heard about the Arma di Taggia scheme and, like ourselves, were hopeful of using the occasion to get back to their units.

The six of us were allocated a stone hut on a wooded mountainside, higher up than most of the others scattered around the area. In the event of an enemy attack from below, we reckoned to be well placed in any scramble to escape. But the two-week period prior to the Arma di Taggia landings proved to be a quiet interlude. We did not attract the attentions of the enemy so, hopefully, they were unaware of our presence and plans.

* * *

Our hut had the luxury of a watertight roof and some straw for sleeping on. A makeshift fireplace in one corner enabled us to cook our food and keep warm. Rations were delivered daily, but water was scarce as there were few streams. We managed an occasional wash and a less frequent shave, having just one razor between us. We lived and slept in one set of clothes, which quickly became lice-ridden. Sleeping rough outside or in places such as barns, while utilizing any old clothing or blankets for warmth at night, left no escape for anyone from this scourge. Yet on the whole we remained remarkably healthy. Occasional rheumatic twinges in one's joints were not uncommon – probably the result of over-exposure to damp. Erickson joked that he would be able, one day, to tell the old folks when the storms were coming – otherwise, minor ailments like influenza came and went easily. There was no medicine.

We passed the daylight hours exercising in the hills and foraging for fuel in the woods. The evenings we spent grouped around the fire, chatting. Erickson and Klemme, the newcomers, were cheerful company, but Ricky and Reg seemed capable only of moaning or boasting. Ricky foolishly carried about with him photographs taken in earlier days of himself with armed partisans. 'To show the folks back home', he said.

He had been the co-pilot of a bomber which had been hit, killing the first pilot. Ricky bailed out and was the sole survivor. Our colleagues suspected this played on his mind and accounted for his frequent acts of bravado and his love of brandishing a pistol. On one occasion he carried this to the extreme, a night when the partisans unexpectedly ambushed an NCO of the Brigate Nere who was riding a bicycle along a country lane. He was wearing uniform at the time so his fate was sealed. Ricky straight away requested the 'honour' of carrying out the execution and in due course did so by shooting him.

* * *

The period of waiting finally came to an end one day with the receipt of a message that the Arma di Taggia landings would take place the following night. Our information was that although some German units were known to be in the vicinity, the beach chosen was reported to be still clear.

The next day our group set off in the early afternoon as we estimated it would be a ten-hour journey on foot to reach the coast, avoiding all roads and inhabited areas. By dusk we were more than half way, where we joined forces with a second party of men selected for the mission. A senior partisan commander then briefed us all before despatching us on the last stage.

The plan was simple. A Royal Navy submarine would surface as near to the coastline as safety allowed and launch its rubber dinghies loaded with supplies. These would then head silently for the appointed rendezvous at the beach. A group of twenty partisans would be waiting to collect and carry the supplies back to their strongholds in the mountains. Meanwhile, the Americans and ourselves were to board the returning dinghies and make for the submarine.

* * *

We followed a carefully chosen route on which sentries had been posted at intervals in advance. As we reached each sentry we were given clearance before proceeding to the next. We must have been within a few miles of the sea when we heard the distinct throb of a ship's engine. We did not know what to make of this, since it would have been unusual for the enemy to be cruising around. We trusted it was not one of ours exposing itself like this just now. We pressed on.

The last part of our journey, negotiating the built-up coastal region, was the most hazardous. It included crossing the wide, stony, semi-dry riverbed. The pitch darkness was our only protection but it made it difficult for us to avoid making a noise or getting our feet wet as we picked our way across.

We managed it all without incident and finally came up to the main road, which we cleared in small groups during lulls in the traffic. The railway was just beyond it and, crossing it quickly, we dropped down on to the beach and crouched among some sparse undergrowth 10yds from the water's edge. We had made it.

* * *

It was a calm night, and we waited in silence, listening to the constant lapping of water on the shore and the intermittent drone of passing vehicles on the road behind us.

At midnight exactly our signaller started operating his lamp, pointing it out to sea. He continued on and off for almost half an hour, at which point the sound of a ship's engine in the distance caused him to stop. This was the second time we had heard it that night, and we could not account for it. We had understood that the whole operation would be conducted in silence. Our eyes scanned the water's edge for any sign of incoming craft, but nothing appeared. We could only be patient and wait. We calculated on being able to stay up to three more hours, but then we should have to start back as we needed the cover of an hour or two of darkness before dawn to get clear of the coastal area.

* * *

Another hour passed uneventfully, but suddenly it was as if all hell was let loose. Parachute flares were shot up into the sky all along the coast from the hills behind, illuminating our stretch of beach as if it were day. We seemed right in the middle of it, completely exposed. Muffled commands of 'Keep still!' were repeated but hardly necessary; we all froze to the ground, scared to move lest we were spotted. More and more flares lit the sky, and then the firing started. Coastal guns opened up directed at targets out at sea, while bursts of machine gun fire, seemingly indiscriminate, filled the air. The barrage continued uninterrupted for some ten minutes and then ceased as abruptly as it had started.

* * *

Neither the cause nor the results of this sudden violent reaction by the enemy were known to us. What was clear, however, was that any chance of meeting up with our own people that night had gone. What mattered now was to extricate ourselves from a potential death trap right here in the heart of enemy territory. The Germans had been alerted to something, and our one aim was to get out of the place as fast as possible before they had time to react further. My fear was that we had already been spotted under those bright lights and might now easily walk into an ambush. But there was comfort in the thought that had the Germans been aware of, or suspected, our presence, they would have continued using flares to assist in rounding us up. As it was, the last flares were burning themselves out and complete darkness was descending once more. We needed to make the most of it while it lasted.

We retreated in the greatest haste from the danger of the open beach, crossed the railway and road and, retracing our steps, headed once more for the safety of the mountains. We all escaped totally unharmed – it seemed almost miraculous.

* * *

It was a major disappointment for everyone. We had returned exhausted and empty-handed. The partisans had taken considerable risks in carrying out their part of the mission exactly as planned but had nothing to show for it. Much to the embarrassment of George and myself, it looked very much as if the Royal Navy had let us down by being less than cautious in their approach to Arma di Taggia.

Notwithstanding this setback, the project was not abandoned, and Captain Bentley made arrangements for a repeat performance to be put into effect ten days later. It was considered safe to do so as the response of the Germans to what had happened convinced us they remained ignorant of what was really going on in their backyard.

So ten more days saw us setting off once more for the beach at Arma di Taggia. It seems incredible, but precisely the same scenario was now played out as on the previous occasion: an uneventful approach to the coast, fruitless signalling from the beach, a major German alert along the whole coast and our eventual escape and retreat to safety.

This second failure was, of course, thoroughly demoralizing. By now, we felt sure the Germans must be aware of what was afoot, especially after two false alarms in the same place. Yet the days passed and still nothing happened. There was no *rastrellamento* or reaction of any sort. In fact, our informers reported life as usual and nothing abnormal in the enemy bases on the coast. All in all, a third attempt was considered worthwhile and duly put in hand.

* * *

I thought back on my training days – 'Never reinforce failure'. Maybe this would be different. Once again we set off, but more in hope than in real belief of success. We found it an easier march this time, having become familiar with the route. We had reached a point just a few miles from our destination when we were suddenly stopped in our tracks. Out of the darkness came a group of partisans rushing back from their advanced sentry posts. The game was up, they said; Germans had that evening moved in around Arma di Taggia, and two contingents of soldiers had taken up concealed firing positions on each side of the river bed at precisely the point we had planned to cross.

So ended a courageous attempt by the partisans to outwit the enemy. Twice they had done so but reaped no reward; now they had been defeated by the enemy within. Clearly, an informer had exposed everything to the Germans, including the exact time and place of the operation. But who? Not a single partisan of our group had been captured since this operation was first planned, so no leakage could have occurred there. An investigation was put in hand straight away.

The following day, two partisans appeared on our doorstep. They said they were under secret orders from the area commander. At the post mortem just held, the leaders had been convinced that their Arma di Taggia plans had been betrayed to the Germans by a young woman working with them known as Olga. She would have to be eliminated. These two men had been entrusted with the task and they considered it wisest to carry it out in our location.

* * *

Olga had been with the group some time. She claimed to be Yugoslav and, like most partisans, used a fictitious name. Being a woman, she was able to move about quite freely without raising suspicion. In the nearest large town of San Remo she had acquainted herself with Germans and, from time to time, brought back information of use to the partisans. She was the only one who had been in direct contact with the enemy since the second failure at Arma di Taggia. The leaders considered this and, together with other evidence, it led them to one conclusion. This woman had been a double agent.

It was realized that the sentence passed on Olga would be far from meeting general approval if it became known. For this reason, and to forestall any possible repercussions, the whole thing was being kept secret. Women were rare creatures among partisan bands, and Olga was well liked and sociable – Ricky and Reg both claimed they had been recipients of her favours in the past. Her demise would be anything but popular.

* * *

The two men who came to see us reasoned that our place would be safest for the deed. Apart from anything else, we were high up and somewhat remote from the others. Their plan was to tell Olga that we wished to speak to her about her contacts with Germans. Then, unknown to the others, they would escort her up to our place that afternoon. On the way up one of them would walk behind her and, on reaching our hut, would shoot her in the back of the head. In this way she would have no time to realize what was happening. The pistol shot might be heard from down below, but such things were commonplace, and it would not be considered significant. The body could be disposed of there and then in the vicinity. Hopefully, no outsiders would ever learn the truth of her disappearance. Having made known their plans, they departed.

The visit left us feeling uncomfortable and apprehensive; the usual light-hearted banter between the six of us was muted. The proposed appalling scenario to be enacted that afternoon in our presence left me numb, and the period of waiting was harrowing.

* * *

Three hours passed before we heard them approaching. The girl stepped out from some bushes in the company of the two partisans and advanced towards our hut. A single shot rang out. She slumped to the ground.

A proper grave was impossible – we had no implements. The best we could do was to bury her in a shallow trench we managed to scoop out of the soft earth of a terrace behind the hut. A pair of small boots thrown to one side was the only visible reminder of this tragedy.

That night the two partisans stayed on and slept in our hut. No one had much appetite for food, nor was there much conversation as we sat around the wood fire in the semi-darkness. I felt for the young man who had been destined to carry out this act. He sat cross-legged on the ground in silence, his wet face buried in his hands and his body visibly shivering. He was no thug, just an ordinary, very polite youth who had once worked in a bank.

* * *

It soon became apparent that the recent disclosures to the Germans had not been confined to the Arma di Taggia operations, for on the very next day our group area was subjected to a sudden and concentrated assault by the enemy. They had not been in these parts before, yet they seemed to know exactly where we were located. They must also have learned that the radio team was working with us and would have been very anxious to catch it. Captain Bentley had wisely moved elsewhere already.

It started about midday, an unusual time for a *rastrellamento*. We were dishing out a hot meal when the silence was broken by the crackle of automatic weapons and explosions of hand grenades. A group of partisans came rushing past our hut yelling that Germans were approaching. Their warning was hardly necessary; we were already preparing our exodus. Having gathered up our few personal belongings, we scrambled up the terraces clinging to the side of the mountain and, when higher up, disappeared into a densely wooded area where concealment was easy.

We continued climbing for about half an hour and then, feeling somewhat safer in our elevated position, threw ourselves on the ground to rest and wait. The *rastrellamento* did not last long, judging by the noise, but we were taking no chances and let a couple of hours pass before stirring ourselves and making our way back.

The weather was changing, and when we reached the hut in the fading light, it was raining and misty. The place was deserted – the enemy as usual having retreated before dark. But they had left their mark. Our cosy home for the past month was a shambles; the straw had been burned, the roof had collapsed and the rain was pouring in. The few cooking utensils had been kicked outside and trodden on.

We met up with some other dispossessed colleagues who told us that there had been quite a few casualties during the afternoon, and some prisoners taken. Among those killed, ironically, was one of the two men who had been involved in the execution of Olga just the day before.

* * *

Our group was still about fifty strong and soon reorganized. We moved away that night with orders to reassemble in another selected location. In the morning we ran into a second partisan group. They were much better equipped than us and had recently successfully engaged an enemy unit close to the nearby mountain village of Triora. This group even had a mobile kitchen plus mule to transport it. They offered us a hot meal which, in our condition, we were more than glad to accept.

Serving with them were six or seven Austrians – deserters from the German Wehrmacht, complete with arms and ammunition and dressed in field grey uniforms. Austrians, but not Germans, who fell into partisan hands, were given the option of joining them. Our group had two such recruits for a while, but then they had a change of heart and made off. Before they could reach safety, however, they were tracked down by the partisans and shot.

* * *

On reaching the territory newly assigned to our group, there followed the usual initial scramble, seeking out and securing shelter for sleeping – it was still winter and nights were cold. Shelter was scarce and always a first priority. Food, so far, had been a less urgent matter, as the partisans normally managed to beg or buy it from local farmers wherever we went.

* * *

We then met with Captain Bentley again. He had been forced, more or less, to abandon plans to land arms on the coast. This also spelled an end to our hopes of using the occasion as a means of escape.

It had been frustrating, finding ourselves so tantalizingly close to freedom for so long while our efforts to reach it had been thwarted time and again. From Bordighera it had been possible, on a clear day, to look along the curving coastline and actually see the territory newly occupied by the Allies. Today, six months later, while much closer, it remained, nevertheless, sadly out of reach.

The six of us discussed possible alternative means of reaching our own lines. The battle front was now only 15 miles away, lying roughly along the French-Italian border stretching from the Alps to the coast. But there was little movement – it had stabilized. The Germans on this side were heavily concentrated and well dug in. The prospect of successfully breaching their lines to reach ours was not good. A better bet, we decided, was an attempt to escape by sea – we were likewise only 15 miles from the coast.

For this we should have to find a suitable boat in the right place, as well as securing a billet nearby where we could hide, pending the opportunity to make a getaway. If all went well and we succeeded in getting clean away, then a night's steady rowing along the coast towards France was all we should need to be clear of enemy territory and land safely behind our own lines.

Our proposals were put by Captain Bentley to the senior local partisan commander, who promised to provide all possible help. Captain Bentley, himself, was moving elsewhere and before taking his leave of us handed me a thick envelope with the request that I deliver it to the Allied HQ in Nice if we should make it.

It contained information about local military matters which, for various reasons, he had been unable to transmit by radio. He was severely limited in the amount of material he could send back as he was obliged to keep his transmissions short and change location frequently in order to avoid detection by the enemy. They knew of his presence and were desperate to track him down.

I was glad of this opportunity to be able to make some positive contribution, at long last, to the local war effort. I tucked the package into the inside pocket of my German military greatcoat. The latter had been acquired recently, and I had managed to get it dyed black by a helpful farmer's wife.

Chapter 20

Flight to Freedom

The next few weeks proved to be the most hazardous of all those we had spent on the run with partisans. The Germans and Fascists gave us little respite. The effects of the now one-sided struggle were starting to tell. Partisans were being picked up more frequently, while increasing numbers of local farmers suspected of aiding them were being arrested and punished. There seemed little doubt, judging by the time and place of recent *rastrellamenti*, that information on the whereabouts of partisan bands and even of Allied officers must have been leaking through.

The areas where George and I found ourselves seemed to be particularly prone to search and attack. This suggested that the enemy was acting on faulty information and believed us to be the British pair operating the radio transmitter, therefore a prime target. This was a bonus for Captain Bentley, but a scourge for us.

In this situation it was wisest for our group, which now numbered only about twenty, to spend the daylight hours dispersed in the woods in twos or threes. By evening, when it was relatively safe, we emerged from hiding and made our way to a rendezvous for a meal.

Our rule was never to spend two nights in the same place, no matter how temptingly comfortable a particular billet may have been. But shelter was scarce, so more often than not it meant sleeping in the open. This was difficult on sloping ground without the support of a tree trunk to prevent one sliding. The ideal place to secure was one giving cover from view and at the same time protection from enemy fire.

Attacks habitually commenced at first light, when it might be too late to move elsewhere.

* * *

One night, on reaching the place for our usual get-together, we were greeted with the heartening news that a large quantity of meat had been unexpectedly acquired. Chunks of it were sizzling at the bottom of a large cauldron sitting on a blazing fire. The fire, as always, was laid in a ravine to prevent it being seen from the valleys down below. We kept it well stoked, and in due course, after water and vegetables had been added to the cauldron, ample quantities of a rich stew were available for everyone.

After the feast, men sat round the dying embers chatting and smoking. We joked with the Americans about the luxuries of life. Ricky and Reg described a superb den that had come their way. It was waterproof, packed with straw and considered very safe. They had spent two nights inside and proposed spending a third there. Our words of caution were useless. When the fire died down we said goodnight and departed.

The next morning heralded the familiar sounds of a *rastrellamento*. It was a bit too close for comfort, but we could see nothing and stayed put. In the evening, when our group foregathered as usual, four men were missing – including Ricky and Reg. It was said that they were caught in the den and taken away. We never saw or heard anything of them again.

* * *

It was a few days after this that George and I had a narrow escape from capture ourselves. We had been searching around in the dark after an evening meal and came across what seemed a good place to rest and possibly spend the next day. It was a deep cleft in some rocks on a hillside, with undergrowth around. It offered protection from any crossfire as well as being out of sight. It was narrow but long enough for us to lie down one behind the other.

At first light we heard firing from automatic weapons so knew Germans were around somewhere. We had not bargained, however, on them virtually breathing down our necks. Unknown to us, there was a track just above our hideout, and before long, Germans approached with a horse and cart and halted near enough for us to hear them talking quite plainly. In fact, they set up a machine gun post just yards above our heads and fired a couple of practice bursts before settling down. Presumably they were hoping to identify targets in the valley below. George and I used sign language to converse, scared to move lest we dislodge a stone or something. They remained all morning up on the road but, fortunately, did not choose to roam about the place. At midday they packed up and cleared off. It was a great relief to be able to stand up and stretch our cramped limbs. It was pure luck that the spot we had chosen to hide in just happened to be obscured from the track above. It was a close shave!

* * *

That night, when we met up with the others as planned in a local village, we discovered that the Germans had been there during the day. They had taken back with them the mule of one farmer whom they accused of helping partisans. They also stole a quantity of animal fodder and, for good measure, burned down a stable before leaving. Despite this, the partisans were still given food. I happened to be feeling too ill at the time to eat the dry food offered, but a kindly woman, on learning this, prepared me a bowl of hot chicken broth. I never ceased to wonder at the courage, patience and loyalty of these poor country people so often caught in the middle.

We tried to minimize these confrontations with the enemy by moving on to new locations whenever possible. There were days when no one threatened us and we were able to relax and enjoy the Riviera's winter sunshine. It was a chance to air damp clothes and search them for lice. On one such day we happened to find a shallow mountain pool with a gentle cascade above it, stripped off and enjoyed an ice-cold shower.

One always felt uneasy, however, being undressed and especially without boots. We had acquired the mentality of wild animals, constantly on the alert and ready to escape at the first sign of danger. Our American colleague, Klemme, said he had been an ardent blood sportsman before the war but vowed never to hunt an animal again.

* * *

With the object of eventually making our way to the coast, we and the two Americans moved on and joined a neighbouring partisan band. Its leader assigned a section of five men to George and myself and did the same for Klemme and Erickson. He felt we should be safer like this.

Our five were led by a tall, jovial character called Orazio. They were a happy lot and we enjoyed their company. The morale of partisans generally was remarkably high considering the wretched conditions they had to endure. It compared favourably, in my own experience, with that of trained British soldiers on active service. It must be remembered, too, that they were forever being threatened, in enemy radio broadcasts and by pamphlets dropped from planes, with facing execution if they failed to surrender voluntarily. There was also a constant threat to their families. News of Allied successes in battle was always heartening. In this respect, the radio broadcasts from London played a vital part in ensuring such information reached the local population. The pamphlets dropped by the RAF were less significant.

The first few nights with Orazio's section were spent outside in the cold, but then the chance discovery of a well-concealed stone hut with a good roof and plenty of straw enabled us to spend a night in the greatest comfort and warmth. Much against our avowed principles, we returned there to sleep for a second night.

On the third evening, when we finished our meal, we sat around the fire chatting and discussed the suggestion that we return to the same hut again. The enemy had not disturbed us since our arrival in these parts, so the section decided in favour.

While making our way back to the hut in the darkness, I started to have second thoughts about the wisdom of what we were doing and put this to George. He said he had exactly the same doubts, and we decided there and then not to go on. We interrupted Orazio, who was leading the way, to tell him of our change of mind. He and the others, however, were still keen to return to the hut as planned. So we bade them goodnight and turned back, while they continued on their way.

* * *

We crossed to the other side of the valley, climbed up a slope on to a ridge and settled down for the night under some bushes. It was cold, and sleep was elusive. Time dragged, and we watched the gradual approach of dawn, hoping for a warmer day. Suddenly the silence was shattered by three explosions like hand grenades, accompanied by shouts and screams.

Then followed bursts of machine gun fire. We judged them to be only a few hundred yards away. When the firing ceased we could hear excited voices, but after a while they died away. For the rest of the day there was peace and quiet.

As darkness fell, we made our way to the pre-arranged meeting place wondering what we should find. Our worst fears were confirmed. Early that morning, the enemy had approached and surrounded a stone hut in our area. Hand grenades had been thrown into the window openings, and as the terrified occupants stumbled through the doorway attempting to escape they had been gunned down by waiting soldiers. The bodies were then thrown back into the hut and left. The tragic victims were Orazio and his section. That evening's gathering was sombre and subdued. No one had much appetite for food. We warmed ourselves by the fire for an hour or so until it burned out and then drifted back to the woods.

The next morning passed peacefully and without incident – the enemy had chosen to stay away. But later that day, the silence was broken by the sudden piercing screams of a woman some distance away. They continued incessantly for almost half an hour, only diminishing as she moved away from the area and out of our hearing. That night, we learned that it had been the mother of Orazio. She lived down in one of the valleys and, on hearing news of the deaths, had come up to identify her son. I shall never forget the cries of anguish of that poor woman.

* * *

The prospect of escaping by sea still occupied our minds, and we decided to press ahead, as soon as possible, with our plans to secure a boat, row along the coast and, hopefully, reach Allied lines at Monte Carlo. So with the help of partisan guides, we and the two Americans moved cautiously south-westwards from the mountains towards a point on the coast close to the German front from which we hoped to make our escape. On our way we were joined by a Free French pilot whose plane had just been shot down. He had baled out on this side of the front but had managed to evade capture and was picked up by partisans. Now we were five.

Converging on our final destination on the coast, just behind enemy lines, was like entering the lion's den itself. We were also close enough to be on the receiving end of overshoots from our own artillery. It was this shelling that had induced many local inhabitants to evacuate the area, leaving buildings empty. Our destination was a house standing alone on some low ground in an agricultural region, the family home of a partisan called Achille. It was behind the small seaside town of Vallecrosia and just a few hundred yards from the beach. It was not a place the enemy would expect to find partisans so, provided we took care, we felt it would be safe, at least for a brief stay.

* * *

Finding a boat was the next task. There was nothing on the beaches – all craft had been ordered inland by the authorities. After a couple of nights scouring the neighbourhood, a suitable boat was found and brought across to our place. It looked seaworthy and, hopefully, large enough. There would now be nine of us. Four Italians had joined us – marked men who were being hunted down by the Fascists. This could be their chance to escape the clutches of the enemy altogether.

There was one major obstacle between our house and the beach – a railway embankment – and to manhandle a boat down to the sea we should need to make use of the narrow pedestrian tunnel passing under it at Vallecrosia. It was the only tunnel giving access to the beach in these parts and was guarded at night by Italian militiamen under German command. By good fortune, one of their number had been in league with partisans, so if he could arrange to be on duty there at the right time, then we should have no problem. He was duly contacted, and within two days all arrangements were in hand and we were set to go.

* * *

It was near midnight and there was a small hazy moon. To minimize noise we had slung our boots about our necks and replaced them with strips of blanket tied to our feet. The boat was no lightweight, but we had sufficient hands to lift it and start the long haul to the sea.

We negotiated the boat as quietly as we could through gardens and along paths until we reached the vicinity of the main road in the built-up area of Vallecrosia. The place, of course, was blacked out. There was no one to be seen; the only sign of life was an occasional passing military vehicle.

We halted just short of the road and rested. The embankment ran along the other side, and directly opposite us was the entrance to the tunnel. It was not long before a lull in the traffic allowed us to lift the boat and scurry across the road with it as fast as possible.

A uniformed figure wearing German field grey, complete with helmet and rifle, stepped out of the darkness to greet us. It gave me a strange feeling. '*Buona sera*', he whispered and proceeded to help us carry the boat through the tunnel and out on to the other side. The worst was over. It was now a straightforward carry over some flat waste ground to find ourselves safely on the beach. No time was wasted wading into the shallow waters, lowering the vessel on to the shingle and pushing it out until it was floating freely. We scrambled aboard.

I was the last to heave myself up into the boat. As I did so, I noted how deep we were in the water – there were only a few inches of freeboard. With nine of us in this boat we were clearly overladen. Two oarsmen struggled to pull us away from the shore. Full strokes were difficult because of the restricted space in the cramped vessel, but they persevered and, although progress was sluggish, we were on our way at last; it felt good.

The night was calm and peaceful, even the guns were silent. It was slightly misty and there was no wind. The sea was smooth with hardly a ripple. Conditions seemed perfect and, undoubtedly, everyone's spirit had been raised by the easy success of our enterprise. Sadly, it proved to be short-lived.

* * *

We had been going for about twenty minutes and must have been well clear of land when, quite unexpectedly, we encountered a heavy sea swell, causing the boat to roll. The rolling increased as the water around us began rising and falling alarmingly. Some of us lost our balance and were thrown about. Finally, the boat keeled over on one side so far that water surged over the gunwhale and poured in. At that moment it capsized and we were thrown into the sea.

There was no panic, no calling for help; in fact, after we were thrown into the water, everything was strangely quiet – we were well drilled in the need for silence. In the pitch darkness one could see very little. It was every man for himself.

Being a reasonable swimmer, I had no qualms about making it back to the shore. The sea swell posed no difficulty and I struck out confidently.

I was feeling quite heartened and reassured by the good progress I was able to make, when suddenly I was sucked down deep into the water. I was still wearing my German greatcoat buttoned up to the neck with six or more buttons, and while, initially, it must have buoyed me up, the moment it became saturated it dragged me down like a lead weight. I realized, too late, that I should have discarded it before setting off.

Still submerged, I struggled in vain to tear it off but I was soon gasping for breath and had to concentrate my efforts, instead, on reaching the surface for air. I succeeded in doing so, but endeavouring to remain afloat was futile. I had hardly filled my lungs when once again I was dragged under.

I redoubled my efforts, striking out furiously to get my head above water. After much kicking and thrashing I managed it and drew another breath before sinking slowly again. I continued trying desperately to tear off the coat but failed. I had, by now, ingested some water, and was feeling exhausted.

Summoning all my remaining strength, I somehow managed to thrash up for a third time. As I emerged, I can remember quite distinctly looking up and seeing a hazy quarter moon and thinking to myself without panic or stress that this really must be the end for me. I think I was resigned to losing the battle as yet again I felt myself being pulled under for what must be the last time.

It was then, in the pitch darkness under water and while still wrestling with the coat, that I realized it had come loose. In a flash I wrenched it off and immediately shot up to the surface. I was now able to stay afloat and breathe normally between fits of coughing but was unable to do anything else. I felt incapable of swimming forwards. I had lost the strength to do so. Perhaps I had been shocked into a sort of paralysis.

I had been treading water with difficulty for a while when someone swimming past stopped and called over, asking if I was all right – it was one of the Italians. I replied that I was in difficulties, so he came over. He gave me a push which got me started. Perhaps his presence restored my confidence, for I managed to start swimming again. He stayed with me as we edged forward slowly until finally we reached land. I crawled ashore and sat on the beach. I was unable to stand, as my legs just would not hold me up.

Those who had already arrived safely were searching around for stragglers still coming in. Eventually, everyone was accounted for and we set off together for the safe house at Vallecrosia. I was unable to walk and had to be helped. Someone gave me a drink of cherry brandy, thinking it might revive me, but it only made me vomit. As it was still dark, we were able to make our way back safely, but it seemed a long way.

* * *

We were fortunate not to have lost anyone, although Erickson had had a similar narrow escape from drowning and after being rescued had to be carried back to the house. The Frenchman was lucky; he was a non-swimmer but had grabbed an oar and came in safely. Just the same, the disaster had taken its toll. Erickson and I were sick and could do little for the moment, all of us were minus some clothing and, worst of all, most of us now had no boots – hanging around our necks, they had been lost when we were thrown into the water. Contemplating our misfortunes, it dawned on me that the documents given me for delivery to our headquarters in Nice, had been in a pocket of the greatcoat now lying on the bottom of the ocean. For two weeks I had carried them around with me, guarding them carefully, and now they were no more. I felt a bitter remorse.

Back in the house that night, we were a despondent lot, cold, wet and without food. The place itself seemed under siege, with frequent explosions around us as Allied shells landed and German guns fired back. We could not remain there much longer nor could we, without boots, return to the hills. There was only one course open to us – an attempt to escape by sea once again.

* * *

The next night, more partisans looked in, bringing food and joining in the search for another boat. In fact, they succeeded in locating two at a nearby repair yard and brought them over. Bearing in mind the proximity of the enemy and their agents, this was no mean feat. Limited work was done on the boats to improve their seaworthiness, and, before daylight steps were taken to conceal them from the prying eyes of any passers-by.

Plans were laid for departure on the following night. Now with two boats between the nine of us, at least we should not be overloaded. It was arranged that Erickson, who was still quite sick, and I should go with two Italians in the smaller of the boats. The second boat would accommodate the other five – two Italians, George, Klemme and the Frenchman.

* * *

On the appointed night the whole operation was repeated. As before, everything went smoothly according to plan. Again it was a calm night with a barely visible moon as the two boats were launched safely into a quiet sea, and the journey from Vallecrosia to Monte Carlo, our proposed destination, got under way.

In our boat the two Italians, with a pair of oars each, did the rowing. Erickson sat in the prow huddled in a blanket while I sat in the stern with a tin in each hand ready to bail if necessary. Our boat kept sufficiently close to the other one for it to be always visible. Monte Carlo was some fourteen miles distant and we reckoned on reaching it in seven hours, well before dawn.

Out there on the sea, it seemed a peaceful world, the only sounds being the creaking of oars dipping in and out of the water. There was no threatening swell to hinder us this time. Distant flashes over the mountains were the only reminder that a war was still going on.

I had been keeping a close watch for signs of water seeping into our boat; sure enough, it started to do so, and I set to work immediately. I found that by bailing out continuously, first with one hand then with the other, I could keep the level of the water in check at ankle level. The fear and dread of sinking yet again drove me on like a robot. I did not dare to rest for a moment.

Three hours later, on rounding Cap Martin, distant lights came into view through the haze. They were well ahead of us and we recognized them as those of our objective, Monte Carlo. We were now half way and it was heartening knowing that with every stroke we were drawing nearer and nearer to freedom. But just then we got a sharp reminder that we were not out of danger yet. A motor boat was heard in the vicinity.

The Italians stopped rowing, rested on their oars and waited in silence. I even stopped bailing – by now one arm had gone completely limp. The throb of an engine was clearly audible, but there were no lights and we could see nothing. Gradually, in the still blackness of the night, the sound increased as the motor boat drew nearer. I had a feeling it was circling us but, to our great relief, it passed by and went on. With the sound of its engine diminishing, the danger had passed. Thankfully, we resumed rowing and continued our journey.

By five in the morning, having been at sea for seven hours, we were approaching the harbour of Monte Carlo. A few lights were visible in the town behind. The entrance was between piers jutting out and enclosing the harbour. We made towards it. Suddenly a challenge rang out from one of the piers: '*Qui va là?*' Our Frenchman was urged to reply but was speechless with emotion. When the challenge was repeated there was a chorus of '*Anglais, Américain!*' There was a pause, and then came the response – '*Avancez!*' It was a moment I shall never forget.

Expectantly, we pulled in towards the end of the pier and on reaching it, abandoned the boats and scrambled up the sea wall. A group of black French troops, guarding the place, appeared above us and helped us over the top. As I found my feet I could not help pausing a moment and giving thanks for this deliverance. It was a wonderful feeling to be a free man and to stand firmly again on dry land in friendly territory. For me it had been an absence of three years.

* * *

The soldiers were clearly nonplussed by our sudden and unexpected arrival, and keeping us under guard, conducted us inside the lighthouse standing at the end of the pier. The guard commander made a telephone call, but it was not until first light that a French officer turned up, took a cursory look at us and ordered us to accompany him.

He escorted us to his unit, housed in the Bristol Hotel facing the harbour, and after brief questioning we were shown into a large dining hall, where troops were breakfasting. We sat at a table and joined in a meal of bread, dates, coffee and wine. Meanwhile, a message about us was telephoned to the British and American headquarters in Nice.

By mid-morning a couple of staff cars had arrived bringing two senior Allied officers. They proceeded with interrogations but were soon satisfied as to our identities and drove us straight back with them to Nice.

Somewhat to our embarrassment, we were taken to the American officers' leave hotel on the Promenade des Anglais. It was a lovely sunny morning and the place was full of smartly dressed military and elegantly dressed young ladies enjoying cocktails and refreshments. As we entered the place, everyone gazed at us in astonishment. It was hardly surprising, considering our appearance: dirty, unshaven, long-haired, barefoot and with virtual rags on our backs. I had the impression that people drew back as we were led through an entrance hall, across the floor of a crowded reception room and out on to a balcony. Here we were served with coffee, while photographers, who must have been forewarned, besieged us.

With these preliminaries thankfully over, George and I were relieved to learn that we were to be taken directly to our own headquarters. After bidding farewell to our American comrades we were driven to the British

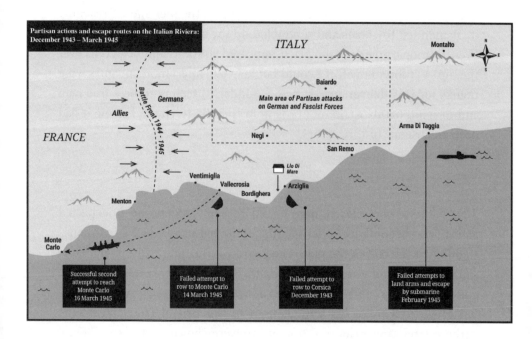

Special Operations unit, situated in a large villa high up, overlooking the marina of Nice.

On arrival, preparations were made for hot baths – our first in months – while our clothes were unceremoniously burned. Our bodies were then deloused, our hair cut and our stubble shaved off. Feeling greatly refreshed and proudly wearing new uniforms, George and I proceeded to the dining room for a hearty meal.

* * *

This transformation felt wonderful, but that night, the novelty of lying on a comfortable mattress, between clean sheets and with a soft pillow under my head was too much. Ironically, I could not sleep. Certain other perfectly ordinary things like making a telephone call – it was many years since I had done so – made me strangely apprehensive. But having the unrestricted use of a radio, and especially listening to music, was bliss.

In due course we underwent the usual debriefing, during which concern was expressed for the safety of Captain Bentley, whose radio had been silent for the past two weeks. We described the heavy pressure the partisans had been subjected to since the Arma di Taggia failure but felt sure that word would have reached us before leaving Italy if anything had happened to him.

Within a few days we took off by plane from Nice, bound for Naples. As we soared up and flew, momentarily, along the line of the coast, I was able to look down on the Italian Riviera and the mountains behind. My heart went out to all those brave people still there whom I had come to know and admire so much and for whose courage I would always be profoundly grateful. My thoughts were especially with the Porcheddu family and, of course, Giovanna.

We remained in Naples for a week before boarding a ship lying out in the bay – the bay where I had first landed as a prisoner. That night we sailed out and joined a convoy returning to Britain.

The first sight of my native land was through the damp morning fog of the Clyde estuary – the place from which, nearly four years earlier, I had sailed out on a sunny autumn evening and taken my last look at home.

Postscript

Brigadier David Ross CBE

My father recounted to me several events and stories from his time in Italy. One of the saddest for him was the execution of Renato Brunati, the first partisan he met. He was arrested in 1944, taken to a prison in Genoa and, together with other hostages, executed by firing squad. His name is now inscribed on a memorial erected in Bordighera to the partisans of the area who died fighting fascism and the Germans. Brunati's girlfriend, Lina Meifrett, was also arrested and was deported to Germany, where she suffered the horrors of a labour camp before finally escaping and making her way back to Italy.

Vincenzo, Elio and Federico, who had attempted to row to Corsica with my father and George Bell, all survived the war. Federico, though, had a miraculous escape. He was caught with five other partisans in the Piedmont region and taken to some woods to be shot. The shootings were duly carried out, and all but Federico died instantly. He fell to the ground shot in the shoulder and neck and was left for dead along with the others. But he was not fatally wounded and that night summoned the strength to escape. He recovered and rejoined the partisans. Vincenzo crossed the lines, enlisted in the Italian Division of the British Eighth Army and fought in the successful operation against the Germans on the Gothic Line. Federico emigrated to Venezuela, but both he and Vincenzo were to remain close friends of the Porcheddu family.

My father's fellow prisoners of earlier days had mixed fortunes. Most of his brother officers of the Welch Regiment, whom he had left behind in Padula when he was transferred to Fontanellato, were taken by the retreating German forces and remained in German PoW camps until the end of the war. Among the inmates of my father's last camp at Fontanellato were several authors who, after the war, published very successful books about their experiences, including Eric Newby who wrote *Love and War in the Appenines*, Tony Davies, *When the Moon Rises*, Stuart Hood, *Pebbles from my Skull* and Dan Billany with David Dowie, *The Cage*. The last was, in fact, written by them whilst still prisoners in Fontanellato. After the armistice with Italy, when they escaped from the camp, they handed the manuscript to a farmer for safe keeping. When the war was over, it reached home; but, tragically, Dan and David never did. They were seen on 20 November 1943 making their way south along the Apennines, but they were never seen again.

Captain Robert Bentley survived the war and was awarded the Military Cross for his work with the partisans. His obituary, published on 1 April 2013 in the *Daily Telegraph*, describes many of the actions in which my father was involved.

The story of the escape of my father and Jimmy Day from Fontanellato, when they nearly made it to Switzerland, has been well documented in a number of books. After the armistice, when many of the prisoners disobeyed the order to remain in their camps, my father and Jimmy found themselves in different escape groups; otherwise, as my father said, he would have teamed up with Jimmy again. Jimmy, who successfully crossed the battle front in southern Italy and reached the safety of US lines, was awarded the Military Cross in recognition of his many escapes. He returned to Wales and to a successful business career.

Lastly, my father's good friend Cecil ('George') Bell, who shared the later experiences with him, returned to Ceylon after the war and there met an American who was to become his wife. They finally retired to live in the USA. My father recalled his extraordinary partnership with George. Night and day for well over a year, they were never out of each other's company. Despite the strains and stresses of those eventful times my father could not remember a cross word ever passing between them. A reception centre for former prisoners of war in southern England was where they finally said goodbye and went their different ways. My father said he felt a distinct void as he travelled home by himself. After a period of leave, they rejoined their respective regiments, George, the Highland Light Infantry and my father, the Welch Regiment.

My father had been back with the Army for only a few months when hostilities ceased not only in Europe but also in the Far East. He returned to Italy in 1946 and to Bordighera, where he and my mother, Giovanna, the daughter of Beppe Porcheddu who had helped my father and George

Bell, were married that year. The wedding, by special permission, took place in the Porcheddu family villa, Llo di Mare. It was to be a double wedding as my mother's twin sister, Ninilla, was married at the same time to Captain Philip Garigue – also a British officer. He had been assigned to the area after the liberation to liaise with the civilian authorities in re-establishing local government. While engaged on this, he came into close contact with Beppe, who had previously been requested to participate in local civic matters.

My father died in 2012 and his obituary, published in the *Daily Telegraph* on 15 April 2012, describes his amazing story and the courage of Beppe Porcheddu. In 2015 the *Daily Telegraph Military Obituaries Book Three* was published and included the obituary. In the introduction, David Twiston Davies, no doubt struck by the fairy-tale ending of the story with my father's marriage to Giovanna, describes it as 'the most charming tale' in the book.[1] The whole Porcheddu family survived the war safely, but unfortunately for them the story did not end with the fairy-tale marriage of my parents, and subsequent events were to cast a long shadow over the family.

The end of the war must have been an incredible relief to Beppe Porcheddu and his family. He was now able to concentrate on the sales side of his work and started to organize exhibitions once again. Then on 27 December 1947 something happened which was to change the lives of the Porcheddu family for ever. Whilst in Rome arranging an exhibition of his art, Beppe disappeared. He was aged only forty-nine. In his book my father does not mention this momentous and shocking event, perhaps out of consideration for the feelings of the Porcheddu family.

No satisfactory explanation of Beppe's disappearance has ever emerged. Beppe and Rita's marriage appeared to everyone to be a happy one. Their twin daughters, Giovanna and Ninilla, now married, gave birth to their first children in Allied-occupied Austria, where my father and his brother-in-law were stationed. Beppe and Rita visited both families and saw their first grandchildren. For Beppe, the journey could not have been

---

1. David Twiston Davies, *The Daily Telegraph Military Obituaries Book Three*, (London: Grub Street 2015).

easy, given his disability. If perhaps he was saying a final farewell to his family, it was certainly not apparent.

After the visit, Beppe returned alone to Bordighera, Rita remained in Austria with her daughters. The day after Beppe's return to Italy, he wrote a letter to Rita dated 16 December 1947.[2] He describes his insomnia, a great sense of melancholy and depression. He ate in a restaurant to 'avoid the voices in the kitchen'. He describes life as being neither interesting nor engaging, but says that his focus is on his forthcoming art exhibition in Rome. He even suggests that Rita should stay longer in Austria with their daughters in order to avoid his melancholy. He is resentful of his wretched mood but ends his letter affectionately towards Rita, wishing her serene days and saying that he will write again soon.

On 18 December Beppe sent a letter[3] to his sister Ambrogia that may have been a cryptic farewell and a prelude to his disappearance. In it he writes, 'Life is a continual betrayal. The most beautiful dreams remain dreams. Who knows when we will meet again?' The next day, Beppe took the train to Rome. He stayed with an old friend, Piero Giacometti, a well-known Italian author who was organizing the exhibition of Beppe's paintings. They spent Christmas together, and on 27 December Beppe said he was going out to undertake some business. He was never seen again. He left his cane, without which he would have been unable to walk far, and also his passport in his room. He also left a letter addressed to Rita. A bolt out of the blue, Rita was to find its contents incomprehensible and struggled to understand his motives. He wrote that he was leaving and not to look for him. He referred to his daughters' new lives with their husbands and families and his son's career as a violinist. The implication was that he had carried out his fatherly duties. But this was hardly an adequate explanation.

The search for Beppe was thorough. The family and friends followed up all possible leads, extensive police searches were made, his disappearance was well covered in the press and the length of the Tiber was searched. Rita found his disappearance nearly impossible to deal with. She used to go to a tavern in Turin, where they used to meet secretly in the very early

---

2. Letter Beppe Porcheddu to his wife, Rita, 16 December 1947, *Porcheddu Archive.*
3. Letter Beppe Porcheddu to his sister, Ambrogia, 18 December 1947.

days of their friendship, and point to the table where they used to sit. She hoped that one day she would find him just sitting there, waiting for her.

Rita also visited Padre Pio (1887–1968), the Capuchin friar, stigmatist and mystic (canonized by Pope John Paul II in 2002). She had discovered that Beppe had gone to visit him some months before. When Rita met Padre Pio he told her not to look for Beppe. He said he thought he was still alive and would one day return. Rita continued to hope for many years.

One theory was that he had taken refuge in a monastery. Curiously, one near Rome had leaflets with drawings on them in a style similar to that of Beppe's. The Porcheddu family and friends visited the monastery, but the monks denied having seen him. It was well known, however, that monasteries took in people, especially those suffering from a spiritual crisis, and would never reveal a name without permission. The family was to cling to this theory. It may have suited them emotionally and even given some comfort.

One of the many famous people who knew Beppe, as they were both part of the anti-fascist group in the area, was Italo Calvino (1923–1985), Italy's most important post-war novelist and literary critic. Calvino fought as a partisan, and his battalion was part of the Garibaldi Division commanded by Vittorio (Vittò) Guglielmo. This was the same partisan leader who had interrogated my father and George Bell, suspecting them of being German spies.

In a letter from Calvino of 8 January 1973 to Antonio Faeti[4] on the subject of the latter's recent book on Italian illustrators, *Guardare le Figure*[5] ('Look at the Illustrations'), which has a chapter on Beppe, he describes him as 'a very refined, gentlemanly, elegant and cultured person who professed a Christian-Communist mysticism and frequented anti-Fascist circles before, during, and after the Resistance'.

---

4. Michael Wood, *Italo Calvino, Letters, 1941–1985*, (USA Princeton University Press, 2013 p. 423).
5. Antonio Faeti, *Guardare Le Figure, Gli Illustratori Italiani dei Libri per L'infanzia* (Italy Donzelli Editore, 2011 p.370–3).

Italo Calvino was to note later[6] that people continued to talk of Beppe's mysterious disappearance many years after the event. He went on to surmise that 'the only explanation one can come up with is that this was a Buddhist-type religious crisis which finally led to his total loss of self.' Could Italo Calvino have been close to the truth? The risks Beppe took in his anti-fascist activities must have weighed heavily on him. Did this burden become so intolerable that relief could only be found by taking his own life? In the case of Beppe, all the preconditions for Post-Traumatic Stress Disorder[7] were present: the horrors of trench warfare in the First World War in the most harsh conditions in the Austro-Italian mountains, his near death from injuries caused by a grenade, his permanent disability, his persistent anti-fascist stance leading to his arrest and interrogation, his work in support of the partisans and the sheltering of British escaped prisoners of war with the consequent risk to himself and his entire family. It is difficult to imagine a more likely casualty. Perhaps there was a loss of purpose for Beppe, with tragic consequences?

So ends the extraordinary tale of Beppe Porcheddu, volunteer soldier in the Great War, acclaimed artist, anti-fascist and helper of British escaped prisoners of war in the Second World War. My father, Jimmy Day and George Bell would forever be grateful for the risks that many Italians, and Beppe Porcheddu in particular, took. My father always said that what he had written about Beppe fell far short of the worthy tribute due to this great man, a man who upheld the principles he believed in, come what may, and who, in his own way, contributed much to the Allied cause and to the resistance against Fascism.

My father was often asked about the debt he must have felt to all those brave people who had helped him. Debt, he said, was not the right word, as that can be repaid. What he felt was a life commitment. After the war my father became a founding supporter of the Monte San Martino Trust, which provides language bursaries for young Italians descended from families that had helped escaped British prisoners of war. Proceeds from the sale of this book will go to the Trust.

---

6. Michael Wood, *Italo Calvino, Letters, 1941–1985*, (USA Princeton University Press, 2013 p. 423).
7. NHS UK 6 September 2015.

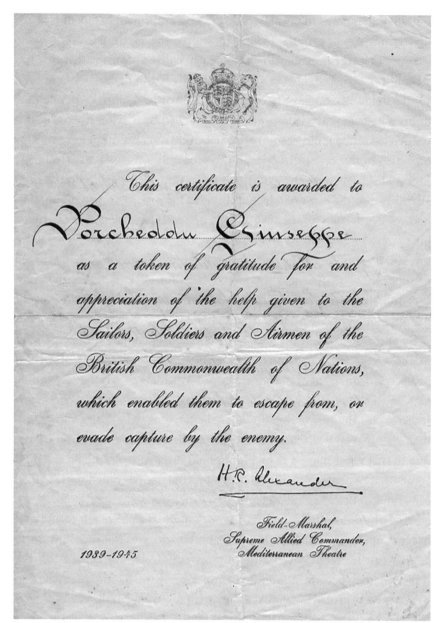

This certificate is awarded to

Porcheddu Giuseppe

as a token of gratitude for and appreciation of the help given to the Sailors, Soldiers and Airmen of the British Commonwealth of Nations, which enabled them to escape from, or evade capture by the enemy.

H.R. Alexander

Field-Marshal, Supreme Allied Commander, Mediterranean Theatre

1939–1945

FM Alexander's letter of thanks to Beppe. (*Ross Family Archive*)

Index